Naomi Pfeffer was born in London in 1946. Following art school in the sixties, she worked as an investment analyst in the City. Pursuing her interest in the politics of health, she went on to study medical sociology and anthropology at the University of London. She now works at the Haringey Community Health Council, teaches medical sociology and is currently researching attitudes to male reproductive biology. She is, she says, an obsessive gardener and devoted to her.cat Blossom.

Anne Woollett was born in London in 1945. She studied psychology at Bedford College and obtained her doctorate in child psychology from Birkbeck College. She now teaches at North-East London Polytechnic. Her interest in the history of childcare and in family influences on the development of young children, including twins, has led to her co-authorship of *Twins: From Conception to Five Years*, also published this year. She was a member of the Women and Science Collective. Her passions are knitting and looking after her cats, Daisy and Tabitha.

Naomi Pfeffer and Anne Woollett have both been through infertility investigations themselves, and it was the sense of isolation that they both felt – in discussion, in medical treatment and writings, and in the women's movement – that prompted their book. Their intention is to add to the very partial picture of infertility that exists by writing about the emotional aspects of not being able to bear a child, about how relations with one's partner, family and friends are affected, about the grief and the coming to terms with infertility. Basing their observation and advice on their own and other women's responses, this is a moving and invaluable account of the experience of infertility.

G000016137

THE EXPERIENCE OF INFERTILITY
NAOMI PFEFFER AND ANNE WOOLLETT

Illustrations by Melissa Lipkin

Virago

Published by VIRAGO PRESS Limited 1983
41 William IV Street, London WC 2

Copyright © Naomi Pfeffer and Anne Woollett 1983

All rights reserved

British Library Cataloguing in Publication Data
Pfeffer, Naomi
    The experience of infertility.
    1. Sterility female
    i. Title   ii. Woollett, Anne
    618.1'78   RG201
    ISBN 0-86068-331-1

Printed in Great Britain by J. W. Arrowsmith Ltd., Bristol.

CONTENTS

ACKNOWLEDGEMENTS

We would like to thank everyone who has contributed to this book: Melissa Lipkin's drawings go beyond the conventional; Pet Smith helped with the typing. Nancy Worcester, Anne Karpf, Jan Savage, and Pam Smith read parts of the book and made valuable comments; Ruthie Petrie had lots of useful editorial suggestions. Penny Facey, Louise Lyon, David White, Sue Taylor and Sarah Kent gave support. Paul and Gordon went through it too. Blossom, Mogs and Daisy sat on our typewriters.

Finally, many woman talked to us about their infertility. We hope our account does justice to the experiences they shared with us. We dedicate this book to them in love and sisterhood.

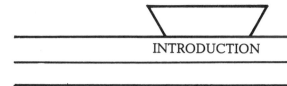

INTRODUCTION

WHO WE ARE AND WHY WE CAME TO WRITE THIS BOOK

We are two women who each decided that we wanted to have a child, but then found that we were having problems in conceiving. Eventually we sought help from our doctors and went through infertility investigations. Although the cause of our infertility differed, our experience of these investigations was similar. One of the things we shared was a sense of isolation, the feeling that we alone were having this experience. This feeling of isolation, we decided, comes about for a number of reasons. It stems from a lack of discussion generally about infertility, surprisingly so, as later we came to realise just how many women face this problem and experienced feelings similar to our own. It stems from the books that we read on infertility, most of which are written by doctors and from the doctor's point of view. Although many of them spell out the physical aspects of infertility and describe the investigations, none of them describe what it is like from the woman's point of view. So while these books give us lots of information about the mechanics of the tests, they do not say how it feels to undergo them, whether they hurt, or are emotionally upsetting. Because our experiences do not match the perspectives of the doctor, we feel that we are somehow bizarre or unusual. These feelings of isolation were accentuated for us because, as feminists, we had expected to be able to talk to other women, to be able to discuss our infertility within a feminist context. But we found the taboos and silence on infertility just as strong within the women's movement. This made us feel sad and sometimes very angry. It denied the reality of our experience. We believe, like Adrienne Rich,[1] that in the realm of sexuality and reproduction, 'it is crucial that women take seriously the enterprise of finding out what we do feel instead of accepting what we have been told we must feel.'

The women's health movement has contributed extensively to our understanding of many areas of women's health, especially in the realm of reproduction and the control of fertility: a feminist approach takes a woman's standpoint, develops and analyses it, and makes this information accessible to other woman. It has proved a powerful method around issues such as abortion, childbirth and contraception. We hope now to see that analysis extended to include topics such as infertility and miscarriage.

Margaret Sanger, a pioneer of birth control, wrote early this century that 'no woman can call herself free until she can choose consciously whether she will or will not be a mother.'[2] But this right to choose is

1

defined in terms of the right *not* to have children. The right to have children and what this entails both in practical terms and in terms of attitudes towards women with children is much less considered. Even further down this list of 'priorities' are the rights of infertile women whose experiences and needs remain largely invisible.

It was brought home to me. I think that everyone has the right to choose, to have an abortion, to be sterilised or whatever. It's just that you're very vulnerable when you're infertile. I don't want to make women have more children. It's just being surrounded by women all of whom have got a choice whereas I don't have a choice. The ones that don't want to be pregnant are having abortions, or being sterilised. I feel as though I'm the only one who doesn't have a choice.[3]

What do we mean by infertility? The different medical words used to describe infertility include those people who cannot have children at all (sterility); those who take a long time to conceive their children or who conceive only after medical treatment (subfertile); or women who, because of problems in maintaining a pregnancy or giving birth to a live infant, do not have the children they want or who take a long time to do so. Many people who think they may be infertile do go on to have children and for them infertility is a phase in their lives rather than a permanent state. But during the time when they think that they may be infertile, are having investigations or are hoping that they will maintain a particular pregnancy, it will not be possible for them to know whether their infertility is a permanent state or not. For this reason we call all people who experience problems around conceiving or having a baby infertile.

Statistics on infertility are hard to come by, reflecting perhaps the hidden nature of the problem. But roughly one in ten couples are believed to be infertile, representing about 50,000 new cases each year. Of these, in 35 per cent the problem lies with the woman, 35 per cent with the man, and in the remaining 30 per cent with both. Comparison with the number of abortions each year (approximately 130,000) and with the number of births (650,000), gives some impression of how common infertility is.[4]

Infertility is a major life crisis. For women who want children but cannot conceive it is a major blow. It shakes your ideas about yourself, about your femininity, and it involves a shift in your ideas about how your life will proceed. Should you decide to seek medical help, your intimate life will suffer enormous intrusions. Your problem is exposed to outsiders and you must submit your personal life for scrutiny and tests – with an inevitable strain on your relationships.

In the recent past, women sometimes resolved their infertility through adoption, but today there are few babies available. The latest figures on adoption show that less than 1,000 babies under six months old were adopted in 1980. Now that this alternative route to parenthood is more difficult, more women are prepared to undergo medical tests in an attempt to remedy their infertility, to seek a medical solution. And most of this medical treatment is focused on women. So a study of the investigation and treatment of infertility is largely a study of the medical management of women.

But the medical management of infertility provides only a very partial picture of the experience. It excludes the emotional aspects, the anxiety that you may be unable to bear a child, the grief and coming to terms with your infertility. Infertility is a personal and social dilemma for women and their partners and for those around them, and writing and thinking about it almost entirely as a medical problem masks this side of infertility. This does a disservice, we feel, to those who have to face their own or other people's infertility. So in this book we are focusing very heavily on these aspects of women's experience of infertility.

Our ideas about infertility came out of our own involvement. So we have started our book with an account of one woman's experience. But however powerful our own experiences, they are those of only two women. We were concerned to discover to what extent these experiences were idiosyncratic and to what extent they are similar to those of the majority of infertile women. So we asked other women to share their experiences with us.

We spoke to a large number of women about infertility. For none of them was it an easy experience, one which passed away and left them unscathed. It was one which had to be struggled with, which was painful and which had a major impact on their lives for a number of years, if not forever. In speaking predominantly to women we describe the experience from a woman's point of view because, although in at least one-third of cases male factors are heavily implicated, infertility is mostly seen as a woman's problem. Women are assumed to be more committed to wanting children and so infertility is seen as more of an issue for them. This is an assumption that we wish to question. But while this is how men's and women's motivation to have children is perceived, infertility is a greater life crisis for women than for men. This may make women more ready to talk about it. Also, it is women who by and large undergo the infertility investigations even when the problem lies with the man. So it is largely women for whom infertility becomes an issue and so we have concentrated on their experiences.

But infertility is very much a problem for a woman and her partner. Men have strong feelings about their fertility and their desire to produce children. Although fertility is bound up with sexuality for both men and women, it is male fertility which is most often, incorrectly, confused with sexual potency. We have not however attempted to tap directly or systematically men's reactions to infertility. By talking to their partners, we have of course tapped many of their feelings and reactions indirectly. Women's anxieties about their partner's reactions to their own infertility or their reactions to their partner's infertility are an important element in this experience. Many men have talked to us informally and their comments have, we hope, enlarged our understanding.

In this book we try to follow the course of women's infertility experiences, starting with deciding to get pregnant and feelings about having and rearing children (chapter 2). We then look at how quickly women expect to get pregnant and their realisations that they are having

3

problems (chapter 3). In chapters 4 to 7 infertility tests and treatments are discussed. We have tried to provide information about the hormonal and physical conditions necessary for conception and for the maintenance of pregnancy, giving considerable weight to the reactions and feelings of women about the investigations and the impact they had on their lives. Chapter 8 looks at miscarriage and stillbirth. In chapter 9 we talk about the ways in which women overcome their infertility; for some that means getting pregnant, for others it means adoption or involvement in shared childcare. In chapter 10 we discuss how women come to terms with infertility and childlessness. At all points we allow women to talk for themselves, using quotations from the women we spoke to. The advice we give comes from them.

This book is written by infertile women for others and so we have addressed the reader as 'you'. We hope, however, that others may also gain some insight into what it is like to be infertile.

DISCOVERING THAT YOU ARE INFERTILE:
ONE WOMAN'S EXPERIENCE

'Well,' they said, 'if you're going to have a baby you should start soon. You're not getting any younger you know.'

It took me a long time to decide that I wanted a child. I started thinking about it perhaps four years ago. I thought about it. I talked to other women. I listened to other women, to mothers and women without children. I found out about childcare arrangements. I thought about my job and how having a child would influence my work. I talked to the man I live with about a child and the effects one might have on our lives and on our relationship. We thought about when would be a good time to have a child. A baby born in the spring or summer would fit in well with my work.

April 1978 I put my cap away.

August 1978 We go away on holiday.

September 1978 Period two days late and breasts feel very tender. Are they normally tender just before my period? I become much more sensitive to my body. I live inside myself, my centre of gravity seems to be somewhere inside my uterus. I feel full, preoccupied, pleased that I might be pregnant. Then blood. No pregnancy. No baby. Perhaps next month.

1 October 1978 Perhaps next month.

30 October 1978 Blood, period, perhaps next month.

Why am I not getting pregnant? I begin to ask questions about my body. I've been taking my temperature for several months and I know that I am ovulating. How long does it normally take to get pregnant? I had assumed it could take up to six months and we have been trying for that time.

People reassure me. Sometimes it takes a long time. I'm given advice, information, details about how other people did it. I'm consoled, never mind, you'll make it. I'm trying to grapple with the idea that perhaps I won't make it. That idea creeps into my mind and I want to discuss it. But it's not something people are willing to discuss. A friend gets pregnant. It didn't take her long. She gets bigger. We discuss home confinements, epidurals, baby clothes, names. The world seems to be full of pregnant women, in the streets, holding babies, pushing prams. I'm surrounded by pregnant women. I read up on conception and find that infertility tests begin with an examination of the man's sperm.

4 December 1978 A friend, a nurse, arranges for us to have a sperm test. She provides us with the plastic container in its brown box, complete with instructions. 'The sperm must be produced by masturbation and reach the laboratory within four hours.' So today, the alarm goes off, I get up and make a cup of tea while Paul produces the specimen (how quickly we get into the jargon) and we rush it up the road to my friend who takes it to the lab at work.

The same friend arranges for us to attend the fertility clinic attached to the birth control clinic where she works. This is the same clinic I have been attending for years. The appointment is for after Christmas. We hope that I get pregnant over Christmas so that we won't need to keep the appointment. In the meantime I read up on infertility investigations.

5 January 1979 Our first appointment. Our medical histories are taken and we are both examined physically. We are seen by the consultant separately and then he talks to us together. 'Yes, everything seems quite normal.' But we are told that the sperm count is not terribly high, about thirty million, but high enough. Conception is possible with lowish sperm counts. Paul is told to give up his Y-fronts and to wear boxer shorts. This may increase the sperm count. I'm told that from my charts it looks as though I'm ovulating. I'm to continue taking my temperature but I must use the official forms rather than bits of graph paper. We are told that the next step is the post-coital test for which I am to make an appointment after my next period has started.

In some ways I feel quite elated after this first appointment. Our problem has been recognised and something is being done for us. We go straight to Marks and Spencers to buy the shorts, feeling that things had started, that we had acquired some kind of control.

7 January 1979 Period begins. I start my new temperature chart on the official form and ring the hospital to make an appointment for a post-coital test. At this particular clinic post-coital tests are done only on Tuesday mornings.

16 January 1979 First post-coital test. Attending the clinic is a depressing experience. A feeling of heaviness comes over me as I get closer to the clinic. I walk past the Family Planning clinic which I've attended for many years, down the corridor, past the row of women waiting their turn, to the door marked 'Subfertility Clinic'. I am redefined. I am now infertile, a woman with a problem. I announce my arrival, show my card with my new number on it. When I was fertile I was E34976. Now that I'm infertile, I'm 4032.

I wait my turn, sitting by myself, getting lower and lower, trying to fight the tears, and the feelings of self-pity. It is my turn. I go in and undress, and lie on the couch as instructed. A doctor, a woman, not the one we'd seen previously, inserts a speculum and then using a long rubber tube takes a sample of my cervical mucus. While I get dressed, she goes over to the other side of the room to examine my mucus under a microscope. 'I don't like this at all,' she says. I panic. What have I done? Hadn't we followed the instructions? I feel like a naughty child and I start to cry. The tears stream down my face and they continue unabated for the rest of my appointment. It transpires that what she doesn't like is the way the sperm and the mucus are getting along. There aren't enough sperm and they don't seem to be surviving well in my mucus. The doctor suggests that Paul sprays his testicles twice a day with cold water using one of those small indoor plant sprays. I don't know how he will take to that. If this spraying is such a good idea, then why hadn't the doctor suggested it on our first visit when Paul was there. That way at least he'd have been told directly. Now it was up to me to tell him. I'd brought his sperm to them and now I was taking bad news back home. My mucus didn't meet with her approval either. It was described on my form as 'tacky'. I am given a prescription for some oestrogen tablets and told to come back next month for another post-coital test.

There are lots of questions I want to ask. But the tears are still streaming down my face and I feel far too distraught to ask them. So I fumble around for my coat and bag and leave, while the doctor talks into her tape recorder about my case.

The force of my feelings and my inability to cope with them surprises me. During the next month I think a great deal about what happened and how I might cope in future.

8 February 1979 Period starts. I feel depressed. I've got to go back to the clinic again. I ring up to make an appointment. Tuesdays arrive this cycle either on day eight or day fifteen of my cycle. The nurse thinks that I should go for the earlier date. I take the oestrogen tablets in preparation for the appointment.

16 February 1979 Second post-coital test. This time I feel much stronger. When the doctor appears and calls my name my stomach turns over. I force it back into place and I follow her into the room. I try to attend very carefully to what she does. Both the procedure and the doctor are the same as before. 'Well, the mucus is better, but the sperm are much the same as before.' She writes this down. I confess that Paul has refused to spray his testicles. The doctor points out that this is quite important as the present emphasis is to get the balance right between my mucus and his sperm. She suggests that I douche myself with a solution of bicarbonate of soda just before intercourse during the fertile days. This may make my vagina more conducive to the survival of Paul's sperm. I tell her that I am puzzled. Should I take the oestrogen tablets for my mucus to coincide with my clinic appointments or around ovulation as the two days are a week apart? Am I undergoing tests or treatment? The doctor says that, as she has an empty slot the following Tuesday, I can return for another post-coital so she can check the sperm and the mucus nearer to ovulation and after I have been using the douche. When she'd got the mucus right, she'd move on to other things, in particular, on to checking whether my tubes were unblocked. I'm even more puzzled. Why bother spending months checking my mucus if we then discover that my tubes are blocked? Why is only one test done at a time? I suppose I'd expected the investigation to be more like an MOT, where your car is given a whole range of tests at one go, and so you know what's wrong fairly rapidly. I tell the doctor how depressed I feel and that I'm worried that the investigations might destroy the relationship into which the child would be born. But any talk of emotions is brushed aside with the comment that some people feel quite heartened to think that treatment is being offered and that some couples are willing to go to the most elaborate extremes to have a child. I take the hint and shut up.

The clinic nurse shows me how to use the douche. She is much more cheery and tries to boost me by telling me how successful the doctor is at getting women pregnant.

The visit is over. The tension gradually subsides. At least this time I didn't collapse and I did manage to ask most of my questions. Now I have to go home with my collection of bits and pieces, instructions and information and prepare us for the next appointment.

I tell Paul what the doctor said about spraying his testicles, that he must do it to improve motility. He refuses. She made it clear that this is the next step in the proceedings. If he's not prepared to do it then we've reached a stalemate. Will they be prepared to continue the investigations if he's uncooperative? I feel cross with him. I've had to go to the clinic, go through the humiliating examinations and face the doctor and now he won't do his share. Later he agrees to try. Our sex life has taken on new elements: Paul sprays his balls twice a day; just before intercourse I pop into the bathroom and spend five minutes with the douche.

20 February 1979 Third post-coital test. My mucus has remained good and the number of sperm has improved but their motility is still low. The doctor suggests I continue with the current regime of tablets, douche and spray. We now move on to other things: an X-ray of my Fallopian tubes. A form is filled in and I am told to ring the hospital's X-ray department when my next period arrives to make an appointment for day ten of my cycle. Via me, Paul is advised to see the semenologist, in six weeks' time.

26 February 1979 My fertile period is over and so the rites can cease for a while till next month. I can stop gently bullying Paul for a while, and relax. My friend has had her baby and I go to see it. I feel very thrilled for her. But after the excitement wears off I feel very sad. If I'd got pregnant quickly my baby would be almost due. I realise how much I'd stopped thinking about children and babies. My goal now is conception.

13 March 1979 Period starts. It is about three days late and I'd just begun to feel really hopeful. Yesterday I'd had moments of discomfort and stomach ache but I'd ignored them till I saw the blood today. I feel weak and tearful. All the strength I thought I'd acquired just seems to have drained away. The discomfort serves as a reminder of my failure. So much for menstruation as a sign of femininity and the potential for motherhood. All it signifies to me is my failure.

21 March 1979 To the hospital for an HSG (X-ray of my Fallopian tubes). I had rung them beforehand to find out how long it would take and whether I would feel well enough to go back to work afterwards. I'm nervous so I've asked my friend to come with me. In the X-ray department, I undress completely and put all my clothes into a brown paper bag and cover myself with one of the hospital's green overalls. I'm shown into the X-ray room and told to sit on a long table with the equipment all around and above it. The doctor and radiographer, both men, arrive. My friend who is a nurse and works at the hospital is allowed to stay. The doctor tells me what will happen. I can watch the proceedings on a TV screen. The insertion of the dye may feel like a period pain. He inserts the dye. It is very painful and the pain gets worse. I pass out. When I come round the doctor shows me the X-ray. I try to concentrate but I can't take in what he's saying. The left tube appears to be clear but my right tube has gone into spasm. I fear there may never be a baby. I am put on to a trolley and wheeled into the corridor where I lie in pain for some time. Gradually the pain begins to ease and I am able to get dressed. My friend finds a taxi, takes me home and puts me to bed with a hot water bottle. By the evening I feel better.

The investigations seem to be taking so long. A day does not pass by without my thinking about them and my infertility. I feel I must go on with the tests, and all the pain they cause, because I need to know if I will ever be able to have a child, and because there is no other source of help for my infertility to which I can turn.

19 April 1979 Appointment with the semenologist. The appointment is at 3:40 and so at 2:30 Paul produced his sperm sample into the little plastic container provided by the hospital. We then rush to the hospital, clutching the sample. The doctor looks at some of the sperm under the microscope and sends the rest to the lab for a sperm count. He thinks that the count and motility are increased, but this will be confirmed by the laboratory test. That's it basically. It's heartening to think there's an improvement. The spraying must be working so Paul will continue with that. We fix another appointment with the semenologist to see whether the improvement has continued.

26 April 1979 I'm in contact with children who have German measles so I have a blood test to see whether I am immune to German measles.

1 May 1979 Appointment at the Infertility Clinic to hear the results of the HSG. The doctor tells me the same tale as I was told in the X-ray room. One tube is definitely clear but the result is uncertain for the other. This tube may be blocked or it might be a technical problem which made it difficult for the dye to get through. My agony is reduced to a technical hitch. If I have not conceived in three months' time, I am to have a laparoscopy. This will involve a short stay in hospital. The waiting list is long so she will put my name down on it the next time I see her, in three months' time. Why do I have to wait till then? Why can't my name be put on the list now? Meanwhile, the doctor suggests I try an insemination cap. I am to return to the clinic in two days to be shown how to use it. I am to use it in the middle of the cycle and then come back to her with it in place to see if I am using it properly and to check whether it's improving the sperm's chances of survival. This calls for another new element in our sex life: I take the oestrogen tablets around the time of ovulation; then before 'intercourse' I am to spend five minutes in the bathroom with the douche after which I am to insert the insemination cap. Meanwhile Paul is masturbating into the hospital's plastic pot, with his balls nicely chilled twice daily. I am then to syringe his sperm into the tube which dangles from the insemination cap. What erotic excitement!

3 May 1979 To the hospital to learn how to use the insemination cap. It's a bit fiddly and difficult to get into place.

19 May 1979 Fourth post-coital but with insemination cap in place. The results seem exactly the same as for the test we had in February. Mucus is okay, sperm count is fine, but the motility is low. The insemination cap has not made any difference so the doctor doesn't think it's worth continuing with it. I indicate my relief at that news. We are sent back to the semenologist for a sperm-mucus compatability test to see if my mucus is killing off Paul's sperm.

12 June 1979 Second appointment with semenologist. We go together with a sperm sample in a little container. The semenologist examines it and pronounces his approval of both the count and motility. We then persuade him to do the sperm-mucus compatibility test which is the reason we came to see him. He seems happy with the result. I feel totally confused. One doctor says the motility is low. Another says it's fine. One tells me to douche. The other says that it's unnecessary. How am I to deal with this lack of consensus? The only response seems to be to feel cheerful. At least someone has said we're okay. I may not be pregnant but any ray of hope is to be appreciated.

1 August 1979 Appointment to see the consultant. He puts me on the list for a laparoscopy. I should have an appointment within six months. It's just a question of waiting. And because my cycle is somewhat irregular, he decides to put me on an ovulation-inducing drug. I am given one month's supply. Am I to go back each month for another prescription?

10 August 1979 We go on holiday. It is the second holiday we've taken since trying to get pregnant. Events like this remind me of time passing.

On our return from holiday, we decide to buy a house. We had been thinking for some time about where we were going to live. The flat was a bit small for a child. We had no garden and getting up and down the stairs would not have been easy with a small baby. When we first started trying to conceive, our plan had been to move out soon after the baby's birth. But as the months passed with no signs of a baby, we put this plan to one side. It just did not seem possible to make any decisions about where we were to live until we knew more about whether we were likely to have a baby. How much longer could

we go on delaying plans and decisions because one day there might
be a baby? So many aspects of our lives were becoming controlled by
our frustrated attempts to become parents. We went ahead and bought
a house. It is a large house – one that gives us plenty of space for us
and for children.

15 October 1979 Receive a card from the hospital telling me to fix the
date for a laparoscopy in the second half of my next cycle.

7 November 1979 I enter hospital for a laparoscopy the next
afternoon. I have never been in hospital before and I am nervous. It is
much jollier than I expected. There are thirteen women in the ward
and we quickly discover who we all are. Six of us are to be operated
on tomorrow. As we have all come in for different operations, we each
have different anxieties, but we are great company for one another,
laughing and joking together. I realise how much more pleasant it is
to have other women around you while going through tests, someone
to share the worries and the news. There are two other women on the
ward who are having problems in conceiving. It is good to talk to
them, to compare notes about the tests and their reactions to infertility.
I realise that I did not know anyone who had been through the
investigations or who is infertile. While a lot of women have been very
kind and listened to my tales of tests and anguish, none of them have
been through similar experiences or had similar feelings. This is the
first time I've spoken to women who've said, 'Yes, they did that to me,'
or 'Yes, I felt like that too'. I see that I've become very careful about
the people I get close to. I am only relating to close friends and
relatives who know about my problem. I feel very vulnerable about
stepping outside of that group into the great beyond of those who
don't know.

9 November 1979 The doctor comes round to tell us all about the
results of our operations. He confirms that I am ovulating and that my
tubes, ovaries and uterus are okay. So I am proclaimed fit and told to
report back to the consultant in six weeks' time.

I feel now as though I have done the rounds. A series of tests have
revealed little that was seriously wrong with either Paul or myself. I
imagined that at the next appointment I would be told that medical
science had had its way with us and that now it was up to us to go
away, to forget the hassles we had been through, to relax and
conceive.

24 November 1979 Period starts.

22 December 1979 It comes again. Another Christmas passes and I'm
not pregnant.

4 January 1980 Appointment to see the consultant. This is the
anniversary of my first appointment at the Infertility Clinic. The
consultant looks at the report of my laparoscopy, reads all the notes
and thinks. He suggests a blood test to check my progesterone level.
This is fixed for 13 January as it has to be done late in my cycle. I'm

also told to make an appointment for a fifth post-coital test to check that everything is still all right there.

13 January 1980 I have a blood sample taken for the progesterone test. I delay making the appointment for a fifth post-coital.

2 February 1980 We move into our new house. It requires a lot of work which the builders have started. At first I organise the rooms around a child. One room is to be a nursery. Later that same room becomes my study.

8 May 1980 I make an appointment for a post-coital test.

20 May 1980 Fifth post-coital test. I have taken the oestrogen tablets for the first time in months. I had a hard job finding them. When I arrive at the clinic, I feel that I need to explain to the nurse why I hadn't come sooner. The doctor, however, either doesn't notice or doesn't ask about the long delay. So I say nothing. I take off my knickers. I get on the couch. It's all so familiar, I feel positively light-headed. A seasoned traveller. The result seems the same as ever. The sperm are there but not very motile. So one year and a half later, we are back where we started. The results of the progesterone test are not too encouraging. I am ovulating, but not very well. To improve my ovulation, I am given Clomid as well as oestrogen tablets. I am also sent off to have a blood test to see if I have antibodies to sperm.

I go away feeling fed-up. It seems as if a whole lot of new problems are coming up – low progesterone, sperm antibodies. If they are significant factors, why were they not looked for months ago. I've had a number of blood tests. Why hadn't these been included then? And I don't understand why the motility of Paul's sperm is a matter of differing opinions. If it is a significant factor in our infertility then why put me on Clomid? We seem to be going round in circles, backtracking over ground that I thought we'd explored. I feel like a detective story, with the doctors sniffing round for clues, going over old suspects as well as checking on esoteric possibilities. Nevertheless, I take the Clomid in my next cycle as well as the oestrogen tablets.

20 June 1980 I feel very ill.

4 July 1980 Period starts. It's fourteen days since I felt so ill so I feel súre that it was due to the Clomid. Why hadn't I been warned of the side-effects? Also, how am I to know if the Clomid is working? No tests are being done to check on my defective progesterone levels. I am depressed.

31 July 1980 Period starts. I've run out of oestrogen tablets. The hospital no longer dispenses them so I have to go to my GP. Since I moved, I haven't found a new GP. By the time I work all this out, it's too late to take Clomid this cycle.

This summer is the third since we tried to conceive. We work on the house. I find out through my friend at the hospital that the test showed that I do not have antibodies to Paul's sperm. It dawns on me that I have decided by default not to continue with the Clomid or with the tests. I feel uneasy about giving up the investigations. Having gone so far it seems silly not to continue. The next test might be the one which gives me the answer. They might just find something that works for me. But then I remember what the tests were like and I feel loath to go back to the hospital and try again.

I feel the key question is changing slowly. I am asking less why am I infertile. Instead, I am thinking about how to reconcile myself with my infertility, and how I can move forward into a life in which children may not have a central role. I feel that this is where I prefer to put my energies, and that continuing with the tests will interfere with this. So I do not go back to the clinic.

THINKING ABOUT HAVING A CHILD

We have thought long and hard about what we could say about women's reasons for having children that may be relevant to the infertile woman. It is usually assumed that the desire to have children is perfectly normal; parenthood is taken for granted as part of the natural order of things. In fact, four out of five people in Britain become parents. The large fall in birth rate this century has reduced the size of families rather than the number of people who become parents. People expect to become parents just as much now as they have ever done. In the past it was assumed that only married couples would have children, but in recent years up to one in ten live births has been to single women, most of whom have decided to raise children on their own or together with another woman.[1] While it is thought normal to want children, parents are rarely asked to give their reasons. Women arriving, for instance, for their first ante-natal appointment are not asked about their motives for having a child and probably few would be able to answer.[2] But infertile women have their motives questioned not only by themselves and their partners, but by families, friends and even their doctors, and perhaps later on, by adoption agencies.

Infertile women are able to express clearly their reasons for wanting a child, perhaps because the delay in getting pregnant gives them plenty of opportunity to think, and perhaps because the investigations themselves demand that they do so. The difficulty for women undergoing infertility treatment is that they need to be single-minded to continue the investigations, and yet at the same time to maintain a detachment from the situation, so they can confront the world with equanimity.

> When I go to hospital, I try to work myself up into this frame of mind, pretending that I don't care that much about it because if I do, then I'll go in there and be terribly upset. I'd feel that the doctor would think I was terribly neurotic, and what the hell am I doing here anyway. It would be a waste of a consultation.

Some doctors regard questioning a woman's reasons for wanting a child as an integral part of the infertility investigation.

> She will then be asked: 'How badly do you really want a child?' This may seem a silly question but some women, in fact, are not particularly enthusiastic about motherhood. They may want a child to satisfy their own egos and to prove to themselves and to other women that they can do it. Or they may attend the clinic to

satisfy their husband who wants children. On the other hand, some women become so obsessed by their failure to conceive that their whole personalities become distorted.[3]

Coming on top of an inability to conceive, such judgements can make it very difficult for anyone to maintain their self-esteem. Ambivalence in any situation is perfectly normal; for all women motherhood is a major change in status and identity, open to any number of doubts and uncertainties.

Goals can change over the time you are trying to get pregnant and become so confused that women wonder what on earth they are trying to achieve. Such a situation is described by Sara Maitland in her novel *Daughters of Jerusalem* where, after many months of trying to conceive, Liz's husband declares: 'But what I hate most is that the more I examine our motives the worse they seem to be ... I cannot think of one single reason why I want this child which does not arise out of my own weakness and inadequacy.'[4]

All infertile women experience moments of anguish and confusion as the longed-for child remains unconceived. And yet at the same time they fear that if and when they bear a child, it will not bring total joy. Most women realise that children are a mixed blessing. But it is the pleasure that they bring and not the pain that is dreamed about and longed for. Adrienne Rich describes this well.

I envy the sensuality of having an infant of two weeks curled against one's breast; I do not envy the turmoil of the elevator full of small children, babies howling in the laundromat, the apartment in winter where pent-up seven- and eight-year-olds have one adult to look to for their frustrations, reassurances, the grounding of their lives.[5]

It can be difficult to cope with such ambivalent feelings.

We examined the reasons given by the women we spoke to for wanting children as well as some of the ideas from sociology, psychology, and fiction. The reasons are many and various: sometimes one may seem most important, sometimes another. Some reasons are felt to be better, more worthy than others. We hope to cover the range of them without assigning value.

Our aim is to help you as an infertile woman to understand and to accept and try to hold on to your motives for wanting a child, to be aware of how the infertility investigations may affect them, and how they in turn will affect the investigations and the ways in which you cope.

WHY WOMEN WANT CHILDREN

Women give a wide range of reasons for wanting children; many of these are rooted in the ways in which women are encouraged to see themselves. For as long as it is claimed that women's primary role is as mothers, infertility will undermine the core of their identity.

Some women have always wanted children.

> Yes, I always wanted children. When I was a child I always played with younger children. I never played with children of my own age. My mother would say, why don't you go and play with somebody of your own age. As I got older, I didn't want to get married. I wanted to have children. I used to think up these great schemes as to how I was going to get enough money to have a child on my own.

A child can be important as a reflection of oneself.

> I always imagined having a girl looking exactly like me. A terrible conceit. It would be something of myself, something very much of me. I didn't think of it as being part of my husband. It would be something of me and my blood and my family history.

The experience of pregnancy and childbirth done well is something women may want. Others want a child to rear.

> I would like to have children and bring them up. But giving birth and looking after a baby is not all that important. It's the obvious way of having a child, but I thought of the baby stage as something to have to do to go through.

Of course, there are external pressures on women to have children.

> Childless couples are liable to a variety of strictures implicitly condemning their behaviour. One argument uses the idea that children reduce a couple's freedom to suggest that married couples without children cannot cope with such restrictions and are somehow less mature and less adequate than those who can... Similarly, spending on consumer durables and evening entertainment, though generally regarded as pleasurable, desirable and a symbol of status, becomes reprehensible if substituted for child-bearing.[6]

Such pressures may be experienced directly; women are asked why they do not have children. 'Where my husband's parents live, they all got married about the same time. Everybody brought their kids up together. They all lived in each other's houses. They'd say to me, "No baby yet?" '

These pressures may be experienced indirectly because of the negative associations with childlessness. 'I associate people who haven't got children with those couples who've got lots of stair carpets and are always going on cruises. I always think it's a bit of a poverty-stricken existence.'[7]

Some women move into larger homes in anticipation of having children. These homes are often in areas more suitable for mothers and children, so surroundings can be a constant reminder of childlessness.

'This is a very suburban area. Being childless here means you are different. I'm not part of their world, and not because I don't want to be.'

This sense of exclusion from the world of mothers is described dramatically by David Rudkin in his play *Ashes*. Here the infertile wife declares in anguish:

> Women. Young Marrieds. Shriek to each other across their prams.
> Joggle their dummy-stuffed spoils of the sex war up and down.
> Trundle along their suburban bellies bloated with the booty of the
> bed. 'How far are you on then, Doreen? Five months? Oh, I'm
> six.'[8]

These pressures fall more heavily on women than on men who often express more ambivalence in their desire for children. 'He doesn't really mind if we have a child or not. He'd be very happy if we did, but it's not anything major for him.'

Children can give women access to a world denied the childless, the world of mothers and their children. This sense of belonging and of rooting women to daily life is an important reason for having children.

> I felt that if you have children you become part of the human race.
> When I started to think about having a baby, one of the things that
> made me want to was that there would be a whole lot of things that
> I could share, that it would give me an enormous amount in
> common with most other women that otherwise I didn't have. And
> in spite of the fact that most women who have kids say, don't do
> it, and isn't it awful, you know that they would die for their kids,
> that they would never have not had their kids in spite of the
> agonies they have gone through. There is something that they
> know that you don't know. It does seem to me that there is some
> kind of secret that they share and that you don't know about it.

Age is often a very important factor in thinking about having a child. Many women feel that it is a decision which must be made now or never, especially women of thirty to thirty-five who fear declining fertility and greater risks during pregnancy. There does seem to be the notion of an ideal time to have a child, when it is 'normal' to want one, and around the age of thirty is one such moment.

> It is something people talk about when you're thirty. You do your
> career in your twenties and then when you get to your thirties you
> have to make a decision one way or another. Other people push
> you, your contemporaries, until you're never sure whether it was
> your own decision or a mish-mash of other people's.

The dangers of declining fertility and greater risks during pregnancy have not, we believe, been clearly spelt out, so women are frightened unnecessarily. Whilst it is true that the risks of pregnancy and of bearing a genetically malformed child increase over the age of thirty-five, factors such as diet and housing are equally if not more important.[9] The picture often conjured up is one of ovaries becoming tired and worn out, unable to produce eggs as well as before. Physiologically, fertility does decline with age, but there are two other factors which contribute to declining fertility in older women. The first is that older women are usually less active sexually than younger women and this means that they have fewer opportunities to conceive. Secondly, older women have been more exposed to potentially damaging agencies, such as infections, contraceptives, abortions, and environmental pollutants than have younger women.[10] It is not the woman's body alone which lets her down. These two factors are also relevant to male fertility. In fact, testicles are more vulnerable to damage than ovaries because they are outside the body, whereas ovaries are inside, protected by a layer of body fat.

Older women may be surprised to find that they want a child and suspect their motives. 'I was thirty-nine then. My first reaction was to think that I was much too old. I couldn't understand my motives. Was I trying to recapture my youth or prolong it?'

Some event in the past such as an abortion or the adoption of their baby can make some women anxious to have a child to replace the one they have lost.[11] For these women, their guilt and grief are such that they believe that only another child will make up for their loss. Childlessness can seem their punishment for mistakes in the past and a child proof of forgiveness.

The desire to have a child is not always there, but once felt, a subtle change takes place which is difficult to reverse.

> When I was childless by choice, I saw the world of my contemporaries in two groups. There were those with children, and those without. They pursued different courses, and different opportunities were available to them. I was part of the childless group, that's where I had chosen to be, because I enjoyed and wanted to continue to enjoy the things that childless people did. Once I began to think positively about having children, then I began to identify with those with children, to see them not as a remote group any longer, but one which I hoped soon to join. It also meant that my links with the childless group, emotionally as well as physically, began to get weaker. I felt myself drifting away from them and in the direction of those with children.

A particular relationship may spark off the desire to have a child.

> In English society, at least, just as marriage is deemed necessary for those who have children, so having children is deemed necessary for those who marry. In other societies, having a child is even more crucial to marriage.[12]

Some women sought out their partner because they wanted children. 'I was certainly looking for somebody who would be a father as well as a husband. And he was certainly looking for a mother of his child as well.' Where a couple have few interests in common, a child can be seen as cement for this unlikely relationship. 'I thought a child was vital to the completeness of the marriage. That we were extremely different people. I just felt that although these differences were a great advantage, a child was a vital glue.'

Some women have a fantasy of conceiving within a loving, sexual relationship, the child becoming tangible proof of this relationship. 'I've gone through all the negatives of having babies. I've done it for fifteen years. I can only think that it comes out of the relationship.'

Not all women live in stable heterosexual relationships. Some women decide that they want a child on their own, others that they do not want to commit themselves to a long-term relationship with one man in order to have a child.

It's always been important to me to have a child. None of the relationships I was in ever seemed to be the right one into which to bring a child. So one day I decided that I had waited long enough and I stopped using contraceptives. I thought that if the bloke I was involved with at the time wanted to be part of my decision, he could be, but it was my decision and my child.

Other women for political, sexual or emotional reasons choose to live with other women and want to share that relationship with a child. 'We had been together for a long time and we both wanted very much to have children, so we looked for a group of men to give us some sperm so we could inseminate ourselves.'

Motherhood is the relationship between a woman and her child. This relationship does not depend on a heterosexual partnership for its existence.

For women, but also for men, children can represent a source of achievement. For men this achievement may be expressed in terms of their sexuality. By becoming fathers they have proved themselves sexually potent. 'My son's an extension of my male power. He continues my name. My parents told me that's what children were for.'

So potency and sexuality are closely linked in people's minds. A child is the proof that a man is a fully sexual person. For women the links between femininity and fertility are very strong: real women are fruitful. 'A child would prove to me, to be trite, that I was a true woman in all senses of the word. That's never been totally proven to me before, never having had regular periods.' Pregnancy and childbearing provide women with an identity, with a source of achievement, one of the few open to women. In pregnancy a woman becomes the centre of attention in the hospital and in her own family. Motherhood gives her a new identity, one that is female and adult. Only in a society where *all* of women's qualities and achievements are more highly valued can motherhood be seen as just one of many goals.

Having a child is one form of creativity – and one which is open only to women. It is often described as so fulfilling an act of creation that women need no other vehicles for self-expression. In fact, motherhood is often seen as making other forms of creativity impossible. A literary critic offered this explanation of George Eliot's childlessness: 'It was her books to which she gave birth, and this left her with no need or space for children of her own.'[13]

Being a mother permits women to behave in ways which are possible only in this context. Newson and Newson are both child psychologists who argue that parenting provides a context in which people can show unconditional love, behaviour which is less appropriate in other relationships. Children are seen as a source of emotional satisfaction and as providing interest and variety in life. Children can be given opportunities parents felt they never had. In turn, the feeling that your activities are beneficial to your children provides a sense of purpose, 'a reason for living'.[14]

The time you choose to conceive is important in terms of life-plans. Some women choose to have a child at a particular point in their career; others plan to have a child first and then develop themselves afterwards.

I never expected to still be working at this age. I thought I'd be at home. My great plan was that I would be at home with the kids until they were five or so. Then I would go back to college and do something I really wanted to do.

A group of women who deserve particular mention are those who arrive at the infertility clinic because pregnancy has been seen as a means of helping an illness: so, for instance, endometriosis sufferers and women with polycystic ovaries are often advised to try to conceive. (We discuss these disorders in chapter 6.) For endometriosis sufferers, pregnancy can alleviate their painful condition but unfortunately this same condition makes it difficult for them to conceive; they may not have the choice or the opportunity to become pregnant. 'One of the hardest things for women with endometriosis to face up to is being told that a baby is going to solve most of your problems and then not be in a position to get pregnant even if we wanted to.' Polycystic ovaries become more difficult to treat the longer they are left, and the same problems face women with this condition.

We have talked so far about the desire to have your first child. Just as powerful are the reasons for having a second and a third. 'It is a married couple with children who constitute a proper, natural and complete family.'[15] This sociological finding is validated by women themselves. 'I've a feeling that a family isn't a family unless there are two children. One on its own is not right. A family to me is two adults and two children.'

There is a strong emphasis on the undesirability of having only one child: 'the only child is a lonely child, the only child is a spoilt child'. 'People make remarks to me about isn't it time you had a second one. I say it isn't for want of trying.' Only children are seen as lonely children who may feel out of place at school amongst children with brothers and sisters. Some mothers believe that their relationship with two children will be less intense psychologically as both can share the emotional load.

Finally, some women want a second child because of ideas and beliefs about the gender composition of families.[16]

Often, discussions about wanting children and about infertility come round to a discussion of world population. Some argue that there is poverty in the world because of over-population, so people, and especially infertile people, should be encouraged to look beyond their own needs to the world as a whole. Talking about population in global terms overlooks the fact that children satisfy a wide range of needs for their parents.[17] In societies where there is little state support for the elderly, and where infant mortality is high, there is every incentive to have many children to ensure that some survive to look after you in your old age. Even in our society, where children are not absolutely necessary for personal survival, they are a source of fulfilment not easily available elsewhere. When work and home life are so completely separated, as they are in any capitalist society, then for many people personal involvement and emotional commitment often find their easiest and greatest expression in the context of their families and particularly their children. This is part of the anguish for the infertile. It is one thing to support those who have decided that they will not have children. It is something very different to tell people who have made a decision to have a child that their inability to carry through this decision is in the best interests of world population and that they should see their unsuccessful pursuit of happiness as a gain for humankind.

3

THINKING YOU MIGHT BE INFERTILE

Having decided that you want to get pregnant, that now is the time, you go ahead and try. Time passes, you are not pregnant and you begin to wonder and to ask questions. In this chapter we examine the ways in which the gradual dawning of your infertility takes shape, how your attitudes and goals change, the questions you may ask and the emotions you may feel.[1] We look at how your infertility affects your relationships, with your partner, your family, your friends, at work and in the world as a whole. We look too at the effect it may have on your sex life.

JUST WANTING YOUR PERIOD NOT TO COME

One of the first signs of pregnancy is missing a period, and so it is your period on which a lot of anxiety is focused. Women talk about the cyclical nature of their feelings, about how they watch their bodies very carefully just before a period, looking for signs of pregnancy. If your period is late, your spirits rise, and you dare to hope that this time you have made it.

You go to the loo every five minutes to check whether there is any blood. You listen to every ache and movement inside you. Then the blood comes and you are plunged into despair. 'Each time I had a period I grieved again. I'd just begun to cope and then my hopes would be raised again only to be dashed once more. I went through a cycle of emotions each month.' Even when your period comes you think that perhaps it might be just a light show of blood, and not really a period at all. You rush off to have a pregnancy test, just to make certain. And the days before your period is due become days when it can be difficult to face the outside world. Some women learn to protect themselves and avoid stressful situations. Each month brings another disappointment. But after the first few days of each new cycle you pick yourself up with renewed hope. Then, all too soon, you begin to count off the days until your next period is due.

With each new disappointment your self-worth is chipped away. You begin to wonder what is wrong with you. Pregnancy is something other women work hard to avoid and yet conception seems to be something you have to work to achieve. You feel as if you have no control over your body and your life. You feel different, and isolated from the rest of the world.

> It's such a personal thing, a secret I was harbouring. My body didn't belong to me and I didn't like it. My self-image was badly dented

through all of this. I turned in on myself. I felt as though I wasn't a proper woman.

Conception becomes an obsession, one which you cannot understand. You seem to be taken over by it. All women who have been through this talk about the overwhelming anxiety, the denial and despair, and the total preoccupation and involvement with their body.

The feeling that all is not going as planned is difficult to deal with. We found that many women feared secretly that they would have problems in conceiving. These premonitions seem to confirm our view that fear of infertility is lurking in our subconscious, a fear of which we are all aware but one which we would rather not recognise consciously. Whilst it remains so, infertility is seen as a stigma rather than a condition which can and does affect a large number of men and women. Indeed, women often talk about how pleased they are to have got pregnant, as if they feared that they might have been infertile.

At thirty-two, I thought my reproductive system must be pretty good to respond so well to our needs. Any doubts I had about whether I could or would conceive, whether all those years of rubber and ironmongery and pills had been necessary, or whether a cruel fate would mean I was infertile, were brushed away.[2]

As it dawns on you that you have a problem you may try to deny it, to escape. At first it was casual and it was very nice. But then when I didn't get pregnant, I thought I can't cope with this. I don't want all this worry.' You may pretend for some time that it is not really happening, and you may try to find other reasons for your failure to conceive.

For a long time I thought it's just that we haven't been trying hard enough. We haven't been working at it enough. After all, I had been busy. Perhaps we just hadn't been making love at the right time. Perhaps we hadn't thought enough about it and wanting a baby.

You may know that for many women getting pregnant is something that happens easily and does not require such effort, but you push such knowledge to the back of your mind. This kind of denial gives you time to get more used to the idea of your infertility so that, as you begin to realise that you are having problems, the intensity of the pain and disappointment is muted. So in the short term it can be quite a useful way of protecting yourself. However, once you have decided that you want a child and you have been trying to conceive for a number of months, you have, in fact, committed yourself to being a mother. You have started to think of yourself in a new way and you cannot undo that. Whatever happens, whether you eventually have a child or not, you are a woman who once wanted a child and tried to have one.

At some point it is no longer possible to deny that you are having difficulties. You realise that if you are to become a mother, you have to recognise your infertility so that you can seek help. This recognition involves three processes.

First, you have to face up to the awfulness of the situation and the strength of your feelings.

> At first you try to think that it's not really happening. But this fear creeps up. This fear that the whole thing is so bad and the feeling so devastating that you don't know quite how devastating it's going to be. The depths of it are so great that somehow if you really open up, you might get out of control and you will never emerge again as a sane person.

Infertility is a very negative experience. However, many infertile women do eventually become mothers. Those who do not may find rewards in other areas so that the pain and the sadness recede. If you are able to learn more about yourself and understand your needs, you may come away from the experience enriched. You may not have produced the child around which your needs focused so strongly at the beginning but you can replace those needs with others which are equally valid.

Secondly, infertility forces you to become responsible for your life in a more conscious way; the progress of your life now seems to depend on your own efforts.

> Taking the decision entirely in your own hands – that's the thing about infertility, you have to know what you want. Other women can forget to take the pill, or say that their contraceptive let them down. They can push the responsibility for what happens elsewhere.

Infertile women cannot get pregnant without thinking about it, or by making a mistake. Because it is something you have to work at you become very aware of what you are doing. For many women, taking this conscious control over their lives is difficult. Often it is easier to let things drift along, especially when faced with something so full of contradictions as wanting a child. How many of us can continue to feel totally committed to such a plan after months or years of failure?

But having taken on the responsibility, you are nevertheless aware that you cannot ensure that you will conceive. 'I'd been brought up to believe that you could have some kind of control over some aspects of your life if you worked at it. And then something said, no way, you can't organise this.' So in taking responsibility, you have to face the possibility that you may not become pregnant. You have to risk investing a lot of yourself in something that you may never achieve.

Thirdly, the fantasies that surround conception, pregnancy and childbirth need to be rudely pushed aside. You have to accept that for you, conception will not be a romantic idyll, but a matter of mechanical engineering. Your reasons for wanting a child, what they mean to you, and how far you are prepared to compromise, are issues you spend time pondering over.

You always want it to be a thing of beauty and splendour, an extreme of emotion. But when you get down to it, it's the other end of the pole. It's just physiology. The romantic bit gets swept aside. In our case, it was a very mechanical thing. You always think that it is going to affect the child.

Many of your fantasies become so far removed from realisation that you are prepared to conceive or become a mother under circumstances which initially would have shocked you.

When I hear other women discussing the right time, or the right sex, or number of children they want, or the correct way to give birth, I'm amazed. I'd be prepared to have anything any way, so long as I could have a baby.

Over the months your goals change, from 'how nice to have a baby', to 'I'll die if I don't'. You feel sad and disappointed and exhausted by the intensity of your emotions. 'I feel I'm hard done by. I know there are others worse off. But it seems so long now. You go from month to month but when you put them all together you realise how long it's been.'

It is hard to bear the intensity of such disappointment. It is hard to work at a goal which never seems to get nearer. Most women lose sight of their original goal, to have a child. It can often be easier to focus your emotions elsewhere, away from the longed-for child who becomes ever more remote, on to something more manageable and more immediate, such as your period. At least then when your period comes, there is some hope that next time you might succeed.

Some people say that if you have a fertility problem you think much harder about whether you want a child or not. At one level that's true, but at another it's about achieving what you're not achieving. Just wanting your period not to come.

By whatever route you come to acknowledge your infertility, and however long it takes, it eventually becomes clear that it has taken over your life.

You can't plan. Nothing holds any interest for you. It's almost an obsessive desire. I became obsessed with pregnancy. I felt like a flower operating on two petals instead of five. Because I didn't think about anything else, I didn't seem to be living my life. I was too tensed up all the time.

It can be difficult to know what to do and when. How far and how long should you pursue your original life plan? Should you try to create an alternative? Should you give up your idea of having a child with all the grief and pain that will entail? As we discuss later, the progress of your infertility experience is shaped by the type of problem you have. Sometimes the problem is clear-cut, and you may be told that you will never have a child. A more complex situation faces those women who do not discover the reasons for their inability to conceive or to bear a child. As long as you do not know if you will ever have a child, it is difficult to come to terms with this uncertainty and plan your future. You hang about in the wings waiting for your cue.

I feel that whilst you're doing it, your life's in limbo. Jobwise, I haven't done the things I would have wanted because I spent so much energy thinking, Oh, I'm not going to be here long. I'll be pregnant soon, it's not important.

Who should you identify with? The world of mothers which you hope to join soon, or the world of the childless? One world seems unobtainable, while the other may seem full of loneliness and selfishness. Either way, you feel the choice is not yours to make.

HOW LONG DOES IT TAKE TO GET PREGNANT?

We often expect to get pregnant the moment we stop using contraceptives. We may have spent many years of our lives and lots of energy trying not to get pregnant. We have felt anxious about the times when we 'took risks', or worried when our periods were late. It always seemed as though getting pregnant was so easy, and the battle was to stay not pregnant.

So not getting pregnant can come as a shock.[3] For those women who do conceive it can take some time. About three out of five women conceive within six months of trying to get pregnant. One in four takes between six months and a year. For the rest, conception takes more than one year. If we take a hundred women who conceive, the picture is as follows:

60	25	15
will conceive within 6 months	will take between 6 and 12 months to conceive	will conceive after one year

Another way of looking at fertility rates is to examine the figures on contraceptives which show that nine out of ten women not using a contraceptive get pregnant within a year.[4]

WHAT IS INFERTILITY?

Infertility is defined by doctors as the failure to conceive after a year of unprotected intercourse. Infertility is not necessarily a final state, many women go on to conceive after a year of trying, with or without medical help. Of course, at certain stages of your life, before puberty and after menopause, it is normal to be infertile.

Between ten and fifteen per cent of couples have a fertility problem, making a total of about 2,000,000 people in this country. Infertility problems and treatment can continue for some time, often for years, so that at any one time, quite a number of those 2,000,000 people are undergoing treatment.

Infertility, then, is not uncommon. You may feel that you are the only person this is happening to, but many women are going through the same experience. You may well ask why so little is heard of it. The only time it is in the news is when some dramatic event takes place, such as the birth of a test-tube baby. Infertility is left out of discussions of contraception and pregnancy.[5] The impression given is that getting pregnant is all too easy for every woman. Hidden at the bottom of tables of contraceptive efficiency are figures indicating that ten per cent of women who use no contraceptives fail to conceive within a year: but these women are never labelled or discussed as infertile.

Infertility as a problem for women trying to conceive their first child is called primary infertility; for women trying to conceive their second or subsequent children, secondary infertility. Some women conceive easily enough but miscarry. Women with secondary infertility, or those who miscarry, may have fewer children than they would like. Many doctors are unwilling to take your worries about not conceiving seriously until you have been trying for at least a year, sometimes longer. Your age, however, is an important consideration.

I thought when I started trying to get pregnant that it would happen really quickly. Nothing happened so we kept on trying. After a year I went to the doctor. I was very conscious of my age. She agreed and sent me to the hospital. She said they don't normally send you until you've been trying for two or three years.

Some general practitioners may just send you away with the advice to keep trying. Others can be more sympathetic.[6] 'After six months I went back to the doctor. He sent me away. Then when a year had gone by I went back again. He agreed to send me to to the hospital but he told them I'd been trying for eighteen months.' Of course, only you know how long you have been trying to conceive. We think that you should be able to seek help as soon as you feel you need it.

IS INFERTILITY INCREASING?

Once you own up about your infertility then the world seems full of other women who have had or are having problems conceiving. Many people wonder whether infertility is becoming more common, but it is not a question to which there are any clear answers. Few statistics are collected on how many people are infertile. This suggests that it is not an officially recognised condition. Seventeen per cent of married couples do not have children, but we do not know how many of those would have liked them.[7] Nor do we know how many single women have failed to become mothers. Individual clinics have records of the numbers of their patients but these figures are not collated across the country so it is impossible to know how many people receive treatment each year. Of course, women attend gynaecologists within the National Health Service and also privately. And there are probably many infertile people who never look for medical help.

Infertility may not be increasing; instead we may be more prepared to talk about it now just as we are about sex and sexual problems, contraception, pregnancy and childbirth. We are less willing to accept infertility as our fate, and so seek help and look for solutions. Because there are few babies available for adoption today, the solution sought is more often a medical one.

I meet a lot of elderly women in my work. You ask the routine questions about families. Those without kids will say, 'I could never have any children' and leave it at that. One woman said to me, 'I wasn't blessed with children'. She said, 'No tug at your apron strings will mean no tug at your heart strings'. That was how she'd coped with the fact that she'd not had children. It's not something they expect others to understand.

Our aim is to open up discussion on infertility, and to give women the confidence to talk more about it. Hopefully in this way we can recognise that other women have similar experiences and so feel less isolated.

HOW DID I COME TO BE INFERTILE?

This is a question which many infertile people ask. What have they done or what have they been exposed to which has made them infertile? There are few satisfactory answers. Doctors usually concern themselves with the identification and treatment of infertility problems and are less concerned with the causes, both medical and non-medical.[8] Some factors are clearly related to infertility, for example, illnesses such as mumps can stop sperm production; and infections such as venereal disease can lead to salpingitis which may leave scars on the Fallopian tubes. The contraceptive pill and IUD may also reduce fertility. But, more often than not, a doctor resorts to a more prosaic explanation, such as tight underpants, often because medical knowledge cannot identify the cause.

Certain substances encountered primarily at work can contribute to infertility such as lead, anaesthetic gases, vinyl chloride, mercury and dioxin.[9] It may be worthwhile finding out if other people at your own or your partner's place of work have experienced infertility. You may be able to collect some data to show that the problem is more frequent than you would expect and this may stimulate further investigation. The Women and Work Hazards Group could be of assistance to you here and it may be worthwhile contacting them. (See Appendix.)

In many cases, no single factor may be identified as the cause of infertility. Sometimes, there may be some suggestions as to causes; there may be a number of things which may make conception less likely. In some cases you may have a problem which medicine cannot yet identify. If so, doctors may describe your infertility as 'idiopathic', meaning that they do not know what is wrong.

If you are planning to get pregnant, it is worth trying to reduce your exposure to potential dangers. The greatest dangers exist prior to conception and in the first weeks of pregnancy, so you need to think ahead. Stop smoking, do not drink heavily, eat properly, do not have X-rays or take any drugs. If you work in a place where you might be exposed to hazards, try to get yourself moved to a different job. Keep an eye on your cycle, noting down the date of your last period, or even taking your temperature so that you know as soon as possible that you may be pregnant. For anyone who takes a long time to get pregnant, such advice can be very difficult to follow. Your infertility may increase the tension or stress you are under and may make you feel even more in need of a cigarette or a drink. How long can you avoid having an X-ray at the dentist without feeling foolish? Monitoring yourself in this way may add to your disappointment in not getting pregnant, reminding you each month of your commitment and your failure. And you may not be able to change your job. Focusing on the risks and hazards can add to your feelings of guilt, blame and anger.

WHO IS INFERTILE?

It is usually assumed that it is the woman who has the problem. Historically this has been the case in our own society and in other cultures.[10] However, as we have noted, medical studies suggest that in as many as 35 per cent of infertility cases, the problem lies with the man, in 35 per cent with the woman, and in the remaining 30 per cent both man and woman are implicated.[11]

Nevertheless, it is commonly assumed that the female reproductive system is more complex than the male's and hence more liable to problems. Women are sometimes shocked to discover that their partner is infertile.

After the sperm count, the doctor said, send your husband down. I was prepared to bare my tubes to the world so I was utterly shocked and amazed. I had somehow automatically assumed that it was my fault because I didn't have regular periods.

Women may also think that they are the cause of infertility because they are more aware of their reproductive systems. Their regular bleeding and frequent attendance at clinics for examinations to do with contraception or gynaecological problems makes them sensitive to the idea that things can go wrong with their bodies. And the risks, however small, involved in contraception and abortion mean that things may indeed go wrong.[12]

Even when the problem lies with the man, it is the woman who bears both the burden of it and of the investigations, in spite of the emphasis on the couple and the problems the couple face, as illustrated by the titles of books on infertility, *The Infertile Couple* and *Infertile Marriage*. The emphasis is on the treatment of women to such an extent that they are sometimes subjected to diagnostic surgery both before the fertility status of their partner is established and even after the man is found to be infertile.[13] Even with clear evidence that the reasons for infertility lie with the man, women feel that it is their problem.

Women are still taught that their identity should come primarily from their men and their children. An infertile woman is deprived of this means of identity whether she likes it or not. While childlessness may be a source of loss and of grief for men it is failure in an area which men tend not to see as central to their identity. They are less frequently asked questions about their children, or their child-bearing intentions and so their infertility may not be so public. While women take the major responsibility for childcare, it is their lives which are most affected by whether or not they have children. Such is the reluctance on the part of women to accept male infertility that they often said how pleased they were that the problem was identified as theirs and not that of their partner. Rather than rejoice in their own fertility, perhaps women fear that they will have to bear the burden of their partner's anxieties and doubts as well as their own childlessness.

> If I thought that there was nothing that could be done for my husband I'd rather that he didn't know. I know it's not so, but if only it could be put across that it isn't a sign of sexual deficiency, if you don't produce enough sperm. I don't think the same is true for women. They can still be thought to be sexually attractive even if they can't actually reproduce. Don't you think we suffer less than a man does?

It makes sense to talk about the infertile couple in those 30 per cent of cases where the cause of the infertility lies with both partners. But in the other 70 per cent of cases where the infertility can be identified clearly as the man's or the woman's, it is he or she who is infertile, not the couple. This is clearly so in purely physiological terms but socially the partnership is described as infertile. More often than not this description fails to acknowledge the dynamics within a relationship. Instead it glues together the man and the woman as an infertile couple; the dynamics of the relationship are discussed only when adoption or AID are requested. Naturally, we search for a cause in our past as an explanation for our infertility. The cause we find may have no medical validity. So, for example, women who have had an abortion in the past sometimes see their subsequent infertility as some form of punishment. That abortions lead to infertility is an unfortunate, but rare occurrence, and, you cannot be certain that an abortion you had in the past directly caused your infertility. Medicine can only point to probabilities, and the evidence available about what causes infertility is very scant.

THE EFFECT OF INFERTILITY ON YOUR RELATIONSHIPS

The experience of infertility can damage your self-esteem. It can make you feel very vulnerable and in need of love and support. But because infertility is such a taboo topic, this support may be difficult to ask for. Other people feel awkward and do not know how to respond or to deal with you, whilst you come to feel more and more abnormal and isolated from the rest of the world.

This isolation stems from the feeling that others cannot or do not want to understand what infertility is like. At the same time, you are struggling to come to terms with all the negative associations of infertility.

It's a very tricky issue talking to people about it. Often people are fascinated by it. But that makes you feel more vulnerable and more upset. Now they know and they'll have a different image of you. You wish that you hadn't betrayed yourself. But you let go in moments of weakness, when you feel more defenceless and upset.

Infertility reveals itself in the attempt to create a particular relationship, that of mother and child. Not succeeding can affect all your other relationships to a lesser or greater extent. But your failure to achieve motherhood does not mean that all your other relationships must fail. The dilemma is that by devaluing or by sacrificing existing relationships in the quest for motherhood, you may become more isolated. It is worth remembering that your family and your friends may be finding it difficult to cope with their own reactions to your infertility. They may feel distress or embarrassment and exclude you from their circle. It can be difficult to break this conspiracy of silence and you may resent having to take on the responsibility to do so at a time when you feel as though you have enough on your plate. Really, there is nothing anyone can say or do which will solve the problem for you. Nor is there any 'right way' for a friend to announce her pregnancy without you feeling envy. All we can hope for is sympathy and support.

The outside world
Once your desire to have a baby is thwarted, the world can seem strangely full of pregnant women, mothers and their babies. You may wonder where they all come from, or why you never noticed them before. At the same time, you feel alienated from them, uncertain how to react or how they might react to you.

31

I go through different phases about whether I can bear to look at a mother and a baby walking down the street. Sometimes I want to stare at them, or snatch them away out of prams, and at other times I just avoid looking at them altogether.

Pregnant women can arouse feelings of jealousy in you. How did they manage it? While rationally you know how easily some women conceive, pregnancy for you is such a difficult goal that you may be surprised when other women are successful. In turn, pregnant women and mothers may feel threatened by you, and make gestures which seem to indicate their success and your failure. 'She said, do you have children? I said, no. Then she made the most extraordinary gesture. She thrust out her stomach at me and arched her back like a pregnant woman. It was a mixture of threat and pride.' These gestures may be real, not just an indication of your sensitivity. Motherhood is one of the few areas where women can derive a simple sense of status. Women do see motherhood as an achievement and this can add to your sense of failure.

I heard a woman say that she'd always been the plain one in her family, whereas her sister had been the successful one. But now she had got one up on her. She said, 'I've got a baby. She couldn't have babies. She had to adopt.'

When you meet new people, you may be asked about your family, or your intentions. It can be difficult to know how to describe yourself, how much to make public. To say 'No, I don't have any children' is accurate but misrepresents your feelings; 'I would like to have children but I'm infertile' is also accurate but discloses far more about you than conventions allow, or perhaps you want to reveal.

If you do admit to having difficulty in conceiving or carrying a child, you may receive unwelcome advice, like relax or go on holiday, or your revelation may not even register. In this case you may feel pushed into a situation of having to make yourself painfully clear. Such an encounter is described in *Daughters of Jerusalem.*

'Well, it is not always so simple you know.'
'Of course it's simple. If you think the difficulty is your husband, I'm sure he'll come round to the idea once you're pregnant. They always do, but men are so selfish ... It really is just selfishness and material greed that makes you unwilling to start on the great adventure of a woman's life.'
All right then, you old cow. 'Actually, no. In my case it seems to be more a matter of my hypothalmic glands.'
'Sorry?'[14]

At work
Different but related problems may confront you at work. What about your approach to your job; should you take work more seriously or should you anticipate it becoming secondary to your role as a mother?

It's very awkward if someone offers you promotion. If you know that you are trying for a family, it's a bit difficult because you feel that in all honesty you should tell them because you might let them down. I keep thinking, suppose I'm pregnant now. I just can't think in terms of a career because there's always the feeling that it might be disrupted.

How much should you tell your boss and your fellow workers? Frequent appointments at the hospital may mean you need to take considerable time off work. Since it is women who attend the hospital most often, this affects them more than men. You may not want to reveal that you are trying to conceive and that you are having difficulties. Then you may worry that if you do tell them your chances of promotion may be spoiled. Women are frequently discriminated against at work because of the assumption that they will soon leave to become mothers.

I had so much time off. But they didn't ask questions. It's very strange. My boss didn't question what was going on. If he had asked I don't know what I would have said. He puts a lot of store on stability. He didn't know I was trying to get pregnant.

Some women give up work or change their job to one which will enable them to continue treatment. Staying at home or doing less interesting work may increase your depression, hopelessness and isolation, so it is a step to be taken only after very careful consideration.

At work you are in close contact with other women of your own age. They talk about their families and this can be a sad reminder of your own childlessness. Their leaving one by one to have babies can make you aware of the way time is passing and you are still not pregnant. 'When you've worked with someone who has been on the pill and she comes off and falls pregnant in two or three months, you doubt your own ability, you feel disabled.' In many places of work, it is the custom for women who once worked there to return to show off their new baby.

People come back to work and bring along their babies. I go along and coo as well, but inside there is this pain that I don't want people there to know about. It seems selfish. Someone has produced and it seems so lovely.

Friends
At work you can ration the amount of information you give about yourself; you may be less dependent emotionally on people there. Friends are different. Their pregnancy and childbirth may hurt and distance you, but you need their support. For their part, they share in your distress and may find it difficult to know how to deal with you. 'I find it quite difficult with my close friends. I know they want to ask. I often bring it up myself just to ease the air. It's a bit like death. You have to bring it up yourself.'

Your investigations may stretch on for months and years and friends might find it difficult to bear with your intense feelings all that time.

'When we were first married, I happened to be known to be very fond of children. It was just assumed that I would want a baby. So people found it very easy to talk about it for the first year. Now they've stopped.'

What can people say? It depends on where you are in your investigations and what alternative routes to motherhood you are prepared to consider. If you are putting a lot of hope and energy into one form of unpleasant treatment, you may not want to discuss adoption or the advantages of a child-free existence.

Yes, you have to get through it. I found that I hadn't got to a particular stage. It was an admission that I wasn't going to have children if I talked about adoption. Or people would say, have you ever thought about not having children? I wasn't ready. I was only at the beginning ready to plunge myself into treatment.

A friend's pregnancy can be a painful reminder of your own childlessness. It can be difficult for her to know how to tell you the news, how best to tell you something which is bound to cause you distress.

One of my friends used to feel terribly guilty about being pregnant. I used to find it difficult to see her which was awful. She was over the moon. She didn't want to tell me for a long time and when she did tell me I was so upset. It was as if she was apologising.

Such news is painful however it is told.

Friends can also be the source of sympathy and support. Once you let them know of your infertility you may discover that other women, some close to you, have had similar experiences. It can be surprising to discover this and puzzling because their infertility failed to register on your own consciousness.

My infertility has brought nothing but sympathy and kindness. Particularly from a group of women who I discovered had also spent years trying to get pregnant. They're immensely helpful and sympathetic. It gives me great comfort to know others have had the problem. It stops me thinking it's just me who is inadequate.

Such reactions can reduce your feelings of isolation and give you much-needed support. By supporting you, your friends can receive support themselves. Mothers often feel isolated from many activities because of the burdens of childcare. Having a friend who is obviously committed to motherhood can be reinforcing of their own decision and ability to have children. Again in *Daughters of Jerusalem*, Liz wonders about her friendship with Nancy, mother of two:

Would Nancy love her less ... if ... she could no longer pity her as a childless woman? She was valuable to Nancy: women like Jane who did not want children, who proclaimed them as oppressors, destroyers of freedom so hardly gained, or women like

Mary Ann who found them boring, not worth consideration, were a threat to Nancy's self-image. Other women who did have children, might be seen as rivals . . . But she, poor Liz, dear Liz, was someone who wanted what Nancy had, who enhanced Nancy's sense of achievement by trying to emulate it; and had never threatened her authority because she had failed.[15]

Other women, less content in their role as mothers, may envy you your freedom.

Some women aren't really sure about whether they wanted children or not, but got forced into the situation. They might actually be envious of you because you can't have children. They might have liked that decision to have been made for them. Then they could have been free. Lots of people have kids who don't really want them.

Family
For parents, your infertility represents a loss: it may mean no or fewer grandchildren. So not only do they feel sympathy and concern for your plight, but they have cause for grief themselves.

My family haven't really wanted to talk about it. I think it brings them a lot of pain. They don't know how to talk about it. Presumably they don't want to upset me. They know we've tried for years. My father-in-law said he would like a grand-daughter, he's got three grandsons. That was just a slip.

For our parents' generation, sex and infertility is a greater taboo than for our own, one which can be hard to break down. This makes it difficult to talk about it with them.

I've never really told my mother how I feel. We went to my sister-in-law's for Christmas. She's got two children already. She was pregnant again but they didn't tell me. I was very upset. I told my mum the next day. She said, I remember when both my best friend and my cousin were just the same. They couldn't have kids. But she never told me that till then. I found out all those years ago people felt exactly the same.

Just as painful can be the excitement of your parents when they tell you that a friend has another grandchild.

I have heard this kind of excitement in my mother's voice, and have often resented the fact that nothing I could achieve could elicit that tone of voice, that kind of lasting, enduring satisfaction. Her envy of her friend is clear: and underneath it, I know, lies a silent, unstated criticism of me.[16]

Partners

The experience women have is tempered, to a large extent, by the reactions of their men partners. They go through the experience with you, but that does not mean that it has the same impact on them. Infertility creates new, strong tensions in your relationships, ones to be negotiated and worked through.

> The original decision to get pregnant was complicated by the fact that I have relationships with two men, so all that had to be sorted out. I nearly lost one of the relationships because I decided to have a baby with the other, and even though I'm not pregnant still, that conflict will always be there between us.

Some aspects of the experience have a greater and more direct impact on you. Others, however, affect partners more, and their impact on you is indirect. So you may be distraught because you are unable to bear children. He may be distressed more by the threat to his masculinity because of the links erroneously made between a man's ability to father children and his ability to have sexual relations. This may then affect you through the changes it brings in his behaviour. One way of looking at the impact of infertility on you and your partner is in terms of responsibilities: who is responsible for what within the relationship during the infertility investigations? We can divide these responsibilities into childbearing, the medical investigations, the emotional burden and sexual relations. Each of these responsibilities presents different problems and tensions for you and your partner.

We have already expressed our belief that for women motherhood is a very central role, more central usually than fatherhood is for men. In fact, however men may feel, they can avoid owning up to their infertility altogether, at work, in their social life, and within their family. 'At work, people ask him when he's going to have kids. He says, I'm too young, and leaves it at that.'

But the pressure is on women to have children, and you may worry that in trying to become a mother, you may jeopardise your relationship with a less committed partner.

> Sometimes I think that I should work harder at getting pregnant, give more of my life to it. But the other side of me says no, make the most of what you've got. I really worry that it might break our marriage, and I won't even have a child at the end.

It is not a clear or easy choice to decide between your partner and your longed-for child. It is more a question of the risks you take.

> If I want a child that badly and he doesn't want to have a child, if I'm prepared to sacrifice my relationship in order to become a mother, what does that mean? I thought I'd go ahead and do it whatever he said. The difference between men and women is that men are more often in the position where they can ride roughshod

over the woman's feelings. Whereas for me to be in this position was a bit unusual.

You may fear that if you comply with your partner and do not decide to go all out for a child, in years to come you will find yourself alone. 'I did feel very strongly that it might affect our relationship in later life. In years to come he might look for a younger woman and try again. I won't be able to.'

So the incentive to go on with the investigations and to try to conceive may be greater for you than for your partner who is often prepared to give up earlier. 'I tried to explain to him that even if I never have a baby, at least I've tried. I couldn't possibly give up without having tried everything.'

It is on women that the infertility investigations focus. Women attend clinics and have to relay the news and instructions to their partners. If he doesn't like the sound of them then it is the woman and not the clinic whose instructions are questioned. You, the woman, must then return to the clinic with the results for which you become responsible. Failure to comply may be interpreted as low motivation on the part of the couple or as your relationship being troubled.

In the 70 per cent of cases where one partner is the cause of infertility, not only does this partner experience feelings of guilt and worthlessness at being unable to fulfil their partner's wishes, but they are also subject to anger and accusations that it is their fault and their responsibility. Because of their infertility the other partner is subject to this distress. Although the decision to have a child may be a joint one, when one partner is clearly to blame the feelings of anger and accusation can undermine the relationship. Hard work may be required to maintain its strength – not easy under these difficult circumstances.

In most relationships between men and women, it is women who carry the emotional burden. Men are less likely to display their feelings about their infertility as about everything else. 'What was he feeling? I can honestly say that I don't know. He would love a child. He is supportive of me. If I were to say, that's it, I'm doing no more, he'd settle for that.'

As a women you may be more aware of your feelings which are more visible to you and to other people. 'My husband doesn't really understand that it means so much. That seems to have happened with my friends' husbands as well. It doesn't seem to affect them so much.'

This visibility of your feelings can be dismissed and put down to your 'less rational nature', so that you may not receive the support you need.

He said it wasn't doing me any good. I was getting so depressed. He thought I should stop trying and channel whatever energies I've got elsewhere. He said it was so destructive – spending all my energy chasing after having a baby.

But after a while, even the most supportive of men may feel unable to cope. 'My husband felt that he couldn't take any more of this irrational creature I had become. I was all right at work. But at home I let out all my feelings and frustrations.'

It is in the sexual arena that the greatest drama of infertility is played out. When you first have sex for conception, it can seem a loving and exciting enterprise, creating a new person out of your love and your pleasure in your partner's body. But as the months go by and you do not get pregnant, and then especially once you start your infertility investigations, sex can become much more mechanical. No longer is sex just for love and pleasure, but you have to perform for conception or for tests. And sex may not seem worthwhile when there is no hope of conception.

> The major problem of going through infertility is making love to order. It takes all the spontaneity out of it. I went through a stage of only wanting him in the fertile time; it seemed pointless on the other days.

Men have to perform; women can just lie there. So one of the key pressures, the focal point of the infertility experience, is the man's responsibility, his willingness and ability to do 'his duty'.

> I regarded my body as a machine, a bit of clockwork. I forgot all about him. I took the tablets, and used the douche, and then expected him to do his bit. He was very, very upset by the whole thing and couldn't cope with it all being divorced from feeling.

Because sex is functional, the emphasis can be on penetration and little effort may be put into making it pleasurable; instead, sexual intercourse becomes something to be got over as quickly as possible. 'It got to the stage where sex was up a gum tree; it really didn't count for much. It was a bit squeaky and not very exciting; a bit frenetic. I had it all organised.'

You may regret the disappearance of this source of pleasure and warmth.

> Sometimes I go off sex altogether. I feel as if it's ruining my life. All these potentially good years are going down the drain. I don't want to spend the next five doing the same.

Sometimes, your partner may find the strain to perform sexually too great and avoid sex. We heard of many different strategies used, such as getting drunk, going to bed too early or too late, working night shifts, or just refusing and even leaving home.

> I had enough pills for three months. The first month we made it at the right time. The second he had to work. He works funny hours and had to go to work all night. It drove me to distraction. The third time he got blind drunk. He said he was fed up with being ordered to do it. He didn't really want to sabotage it.

It is usually you the woman who tells the man when you have to have sex either for a test or because you think it is the fertile time of your cycle. This may constitute a change in the dynamics of your sex life. Some women find it difficult to say to their partner that they have to have intercourse on a particular day and devise ways of coping with it less directly.

> I used to tell him some days in advance of the test or when I thought I might be ovulating. He found it easier that way, to prepare himself and to accept what I said. But I never liked having to tell him. Sometimes, I wished he would just know and tell me instead so it wasn't always me who had to nag him about it.

If you do not live with the man, then having sex around ovulation, or for tests can become complicated.

> All the planning sex took. I don't live with my partner so I only sleep with him when we've previously arranged to see each other, so all the trying to predict when I might ovulate got mixed up with when we're going to see each other. If I suddenly phone and say can I come round tonight, we both know why, which totally paralyses both of us.

Because we do not often talk to other people about our sex lives and especially the more intimate details of sexual intercourse, you may feel that to do so would be a betrayal of your partner. It is hard to cope with feelings of criticism, especially when you may be aware that to voice them might turn out to be counter-productive.

All the women we spoke to had things to say about the effect infertility had on their sex life. They all resented the deterioration and the mechanical way they came to view sex. For many women, having to say when sex should take place is a change in sexual dynamics. It may not be a positive move in the first place but in the long term it may enable us to take a more active role in our sex lives.

GOING THROUGH INFERTILITY INVESTIGATIONS

Once women recognise that they are having difficulty in conceiving, more often than not they seek medical help. In the following four chapters, we look at the medical information available on infertility and the treatments offered. In chapter 5, we discuss male infertility and especially artificial insemination using donor semen (AID) as the main way of dealing with male infertility. We then look at female infertility where far more information is available. In chapter 6, we discuss the menstrual cycle and the impact of hormonal problems on infertility as well as disorders of the reproductive system. In chapter 7, we look at compatibility and the survival of sperm in the woman's reproductive system.

In chapters 5,6 and 7, our major concern is conception. Women who have difficulty in carrying a baby to term or whose infants are stillborn may not have the number of children they would like; this is an important aspect of infertility which we discuss in chapter 8.

The major focus of our discussion is on women, their fertility problems, the tests and treatments available to them and their experiences of them. This bias is deliberate and comes about for two reasons. As we have argued already, infertility threatens a woman's identity more than it does a man's. Additionally, we have more information about the normal functioning and disorders of women's reproductive system largely because research on contraception has concentrated on controlling women's fertility rather than men's. This means we are now in a much better position to know why a woman has fertility problems and, in some cases, how these problems can be treated. Knowledge of male fertility, and hence of male infertility, is at a much more primitive level. So the reticence of the medical world about studying and tampering with the reproductive system of men means that we have less information and less in the way of treatment to offer infertile men. In fact, the major advance in this field, the development of sperm-freezing techniques, comes not directly from medicine but from the world of animal husbandry.

Before we consider these specific aspects of infertility, we look at the organisation of infertility services, what infertility investigations and treatment involve, and some of the general issues and concerns these raise. We also describe some measures you can take on your own – how to take control of an experience which can otherwise threaten to take control of you.

STARTING INFERTILITY INVESTIGATIONS

Most of us have visited a doctor or attended a hospital at some point in our lives. We have an idea of what an encounter with a doctor is like, of what we expect from it, of how our problems are investigated and dealt with. Infertility investigations and treatment do not fit in with our ideas for a number of reasons. Firstly, we are unlikely to have a physical symptom or suffer any discomfort; the problem for which we seek a cure is the absence of a child. So as a 'well' person, we are seeking the help of a doctor who is trained to treat the sick. Consequently we may not fit the doctor's own model of a patient.

Secondly, infertility is a relatively unresearched area of medicine and, with the exception of certain conditions, little is known about it. The doctor may not be able to diagnose what is wrong because the techniques and knowledge necessary to do so are not available. Even where an explanation for infertility is found, a cure may not exist, or where a cure does exist, there is no guarantee that it will work in each case. Faced with this uncertainty, doctors seem to resort to one of two types of behaviour: they may use technical and scientific language in which the patient 'disappears', becoming instead a source of material for the laboratory to test, or they give advice which sounds more like magic than science. For example, it is sometimes claimed that the first appointment can act as a spontaneous 'cure', that many women conceive without any medical intervention apart from a preliminary appointment with a doctor.[1] Women are often advised to relax, to go on holiday or to adopt a child as a means of overcoming their infertility. There is no evidence that any of this advice works; indeed they are more examples of the kind of 'magic' around infertility. Perhaps this reliance on magic explains why the investigations take so long. Doctors seem to hope that by spinning them out a woman will conceive without medical intervention. If this is the case, then it should be made more explicit so that understandably anxious patients have a clearer picture of what is going on and a firmer basis on which to act.

Where to go for investigations and treatment

Your first step is probably to make an appointment with your GP who may or may not know what treatment is available in your area, so it is a good idea to make some enquiries of your own beforehand, informally through friends and formally through agencies such as your local Community Health Council, the National Association for the Childless (NAC), and the Family Planning Association which keeps a register of clinics. You may discover that there are some places which you should try to avoid or others which are worth attending. For those living outside big cities, there may be little help available locally and you will have to travel many miles for medical help.

Investigations and treatment are available from the National Health Service (NHS), through the British Pregnancy Advisory Service (BPAS) on a private but non-profit-making basis, and through private practitioners.[2] NHS doctors sometimes impose criteria about the kinds of patients they see – some clinics see only married couples. The waiting lists are

41

often long so it may take time to start investigations in the first place, and there may be long waits between appointments. And it can take months or even years to cover the whole range of tests.

> I've been to the clinic about ten or eleven times, but it is always spaced out. I go for a test and then I go for the result and then I go for another test. They don't do several tests at once, and they won't write and let me know the results, I have to go for them myself. It's a whole morning wasted. They seem to space it out so much.

These delays may be exacerbated where clinics are held on only one or two days a week. Your own menstrual cycle is unlikely to coincide with these days and so the timing of the tests and treatments can be a problem. 'There were only two clinics a week, Tuesdays and Thursdays. That puzzled me. If you ovulated on Saturday, which I usually did, it was useless going for post-coital tests on any other day.'

Women often feel there is considerable pressure on them to comply with the hospital's timetable. This frequently involves masturbation or sexual intercourse and many people fear that they will not be able to carry out the instructions and will have to miss an appointment. Failing is bad enough but particularly when it can mean a long wait for another appointment.

> It was hard enough having sex to fit with my cycle, but getting up at six o'clock to masturbate was more than my husband could manage. But I found it difficult to be sympathetic because it would mean missing an appointment and prolonging the agony.

Partly for economic reasons, we suppose, but mainly because they are often the least intrusive both for you and the hospital services, the cheaper tests, such as keeping a temperature chart, are carried out first. If these tests are not the ones which detect your particular problem, then it can be months or even years before your problem comes to light. It can be frustrating to know that if other tests had been employed first, then the course of your investigation would have been radically altered. These delays also prolong the agony. It can be dispiriting when, after months have passed, you are no closer to an understanding of your problem.

You may attend the specialist infertility clinic at a teaching hospital where the most advanced, and sometimes experimental techniques are available. If yours is a problem that a particular clinic is researching, then you may strike lucky and receive treatment which is not available elsewhere. However, you may feel that doctors you encounter in these centres of excellence are rather remote.

> At a teaching hospital, you do get the feeling that you are there for their benefit rather than your own. The fact that you want an explanation seems to surprise them. You're there because they are studying infertility, not particularly because you want to have a baby.

Not all hospitals run separate infertility clinics; at the same outpatient clinic a doctor may see pregnant women, women seeking contraceptive advice and women wanting abortions as well as infertility patients. Organising clinics in this way must generate conflicts and confusions for doctors as well as patients. Or you may find that the same facilities are shared by different clinics, each dealing with a different aspect of women's reproduction. The hospital waiting room where you sit can be the source of much discomfort.

> You attend during the antenatal clinic. I'm absolutely surrounded by ladies all delightfully pregnant. I don't think about it so much when I'm out shopping or working, but I'm here because I'm infertile. I find it extremely painful sitting with pregnant women with their little kids, side by side.

The same may happen as an inpatient in hospital. You may share a ward with women with a whole range of gynaecological complaints; women being sterilised or women having abortions. You cannot be isolated from all pregnant women and mothers with their children, but we do feel that more sympathy could be shown towards infertile women.

Not all hospitals offer the full range of facilities for infertility investigations and treatment. Some of the more specialised tests may be available only at a few hospitals. Even where the facilities are available they may not be offered you for medical or social reasons. Single women are denied help at some hospitals. At others, certain treatments may not be made available to them; it is unusual for artificial insemination to be offered to single women. There may be very long waiting lists for some kinds of treatment, in particular, for a laparoscopy and for treatment with Pergonal. We would like to see the NHS provide a better service for infertile people and for that service to be available to *all* women in need rather than just to those who meet certain social criteria.

Given the inadequacies of NHS infertility services you may feel forced to consider private treatment. If you do not meet the social criteria laid down by some NHS hospitals, you may find doctors working privately who are less concerned about your marital status. You may also consider private treatment if time is important. Given the pressures on women to have their babies young, a woman in her late thirties may not feel she has the months or years to go through tests at a 'leisurely' pace.

If you decide to seek help from a private practitioner, you should try to find a doctor through some form of recommendation. Some infertility services are advertised in newspapers and magazines. These adverts are placed on behalf of private practitioners who are not allowed to seek custom through advertisement. Instead, they use third parties to act on their behalf, who will put you in touch with the doctor concerned. Many doctors work as consultants in NHS hospitals and also have private practices. In these practices they may not have the facilities to undertake the more complicated tests or treatments and so refer you elsewhere – sometimes to the NHS hospitals where they are employed, so you may find yourself queue jumping. None of the women who spoke to us found any difference in the attitudes of the doctors they saw privately; paying for treatment does not guarantee sympathy, nor good explanations of what is happening to you.

The British Pregnancy Advisory Service falls somewhere in between the NHS and private practitioners. The BPAS is a charity, and is therefore non-profit-making, but it does charge modest fees. It has thirty branches throughout England and Wales and four nursing homes. At about half of these, infertility counselling and tests are offered, as well as AID. The BPAS has a very sympathetic attitude towards single women, both heterosexual and lesbian, and should certainly be your choice if your social circumstances are frowned upon by either the NHS or private practitioners. (See Appendix for the address of the head office. Contact them to find your nearest branch.)

The medical practitioners involved in infertility
There is no such thing as a specialist in infertility insofar as there is no Royal College dedicated to its practice. In this respect, it is different from many branches of medicine such as gynaecology and obstetrics, neurology and cardiology. This gap reflects partly the historical developments within medicine. It also reflects the lack of importance and prestige attached to infertility by medical practitioners and by government bodies which sanction developments in the medical profession. So the doctors you encounter may vary widely in their background and training, their knowledge and expertise. It is only possible to generalise about whom you might see in the course of your investigations, but the number of different people involved comes as a surprise to many women.[3]

There will usually be one doctor, perhaps a consultant gynaecologist, who oversees your progress. This may not be the person you see at each appointment. If you attend an NHS clinic, you are quite likely to see a succession of doctors, perhaps medical assistants at the sub-consultant grade. From the doctor's point of view, not seeing a patient throughout a course of investigations and treatment denies them the opportunity to follow through their diagnoses and treatments. So each appointment with an infertility patient is an isolated encounter, not one of a series. It is difficult to see how the treatment of infertility can be improved when doctors do not get this important feedback.

As the patient, you may feel that seeing a different doctor at each appointment prevents you from developing a sympathetic relationship. It is not often considered whether such a relationship is ever possible or even desirable. Although doctors often retreat behind a mask of professional coldness, you may find an over-friendly attitude rather embarrassing and patronising, especially in an area which concerns so many intimate details of your life. However sympathetic your doctor, there is little he or she can do to lessen the inevitable anguish and pain. We feel an important issue here concerns the reading of case notes. If you see a different doctor at each appointment, the success of your investigation can depend on how well your case notes have been kept by previous doctors and how much attention the current doctor gives them. 'I went back every few months and each time I saw a different doctor. It was so awful. I kept expecting them to know what was going on but they never did.'

Two sorts of irritation can arise out of misuse of your case notes; in the first, gaps or inaccurate details find their way on to your record, never to be remedied.

My husband has done four sperm counts, but the second one was lost. What irritates me is that it was put down on our notes that we took it in on the wrong day when what actually happened was that one of the technicians lost it. So every time my notes are read, I'm blamed for losing it. I look a right idiot. Each time I say it wasn't my fault, but they won't change the notes. It's really infuriating.

So at each appointment you have to fill in the correct details to the doctor. The second type of irritation arises when your notes are correct, but the doctor cannot be bothered to look through them and so overlooks important details.

I trotted back a few weeks later to get the result of the test. I saw another new doctor who said that the results wouldn't be there for another three weeks. I said, I'm sorry, I was told they'd be here today. Then the nurse told him she'd put them in the back pocket of my folder.

In either event, you come away with the feeling that you are not receiving the best possible attention. It would be reassuring if doctors followed the edicts of their medical school training and gave your case notes the attention they deserve. Perhaps this way, you would face each appointment with greater confidence.

If you opt for private treatment, again one practitioner probably oversees your investigations and this is the person you are likely to see at each appointment. However, in many private practices, much of the routine testing and treating is carried out by the practice nurses or you may be sent to a private laboratory or clinic for tests.

It's like going through a battery farm. You get about thirty seconds with the doctor who doesn't really sit down. It's the practice nurses who do most for you. They explain what's going on but each one has a slightly different version.

Often, whether you are having treatment under the NHS or privately, the doctor overseeing your case does not have the skills to investigate male infertility beyond the straightforward semen test. Where the man is found to have a problem, he will be referred to a urologist, a specialist in the urinary system of men and women and in the male reproductive system because the two systems are very closely connected in men. Some NHS clinics include a urologist in their team, but at other hospitals, or with a private practitioner, the man may be sent elsewhere and this can mean further delays.

There are quite a number of people you may see at some point in your investigations; whom you see depends on what problems are suspected or diagnosed. It is often suggested in books on infertility that all these doctors, nurses and technicians work together as a team which includes you, the patient.[4] The word team implies that each member is working towards the same goal, your baby, and has a clear plan for reaching that goal. Whilst it is certainly possible that each person you see is sympathetic towards your desire to have a child, they may not agree on the best way to go about it; your ideas may differ radically from theirs and it is you who suffers the discomfort. Furthermore, the doctors' criteria of success may differ from yours; surgeons may feel they have succeeded because they have repaired the damage to your Fallopian tubes, but as you are still not pregnant you do not agree that the operation was a success.[5] As a full member of this team, you should be actively involved in decisions being made about you. In reality, your role is that of a client, your job is to follow instructions carefully and you are rarely allowed to question any decisions.

I feel very inhibited. When I'm with the doctor I feel utterly as a patient. I'm very nervous of how he is reacting to me. I can't relax. I feel as though I've got to battle to keep up my confidence and stick up for my rights.

One decision you might wish, quite legitimately, to be involved in is the type of treatment you receive. Some treatments are fairly successful, whereas others have a much lower rate of success. The chances of a treatment being effective may be something you would want to know about before going ahead.

Although it can be hard, try not to be browbeaten; if there is something you want to know, do your best to find out. After all, it is your body and your infertility. If there is a particular procedure that you want carried out, insist – and if you are refused, try to go elsewhere where you might get a more co-operative response. For too long patients have been used to complying with the dictates of doctors. Also, try to confine your relationship with the doctor to your infertility investigations and treatment. Treating the physical aspects is what they are best able to do. It is understandable that when so many of your feelings are focused on these appointments, the doctor becomes closely associated with your emotions. But you may be able to cope more effectively if you do not expect the doctor to deal with your anxieties and disappointments as well as your infertility.

Going along for appointments
Your first appointment is of particular significance: it marks your entry into the world of infertility, a world which you enter full of ambivalent feelings. At last you may receive help, but what will that entail?[6]

Usually this appointment is unlike any of the subsequent visits to the hospital. Not only is it significant for you, but some doctors put considerable emphasis on it as the time at which they obtain particular sorts of information from you over and above your physical symptoms. As one textbook says about the initial interview:

> The initial diagnostic evaluation should cover a number of personal areas including the stability and co-operative basis of the couple's relationship, the adequacy of their sexual adjustment, their general psychosocial readiness for parenthood and the genuineness of their motivation to have children.[7]

You may wonder at this intrusion into the more personal areas of your life and feel confused and angered by it and question why these details are important. Surely your attendance at the infertility clinic is sufficient evidence of your motivation for motherhood? But some doctors believe that couples with emotional or psychosexual difficulties use infertility as a way of seeking help.[8] Or they argue that your infertility may be caused by your sexual or emotional problems and that it is important to rule these out before proceeding with a physical investigation.

How do doctors check that, in their eyes, you have a happy relationship, that you are not trying to conceive to shore up an unhappy marriage? At some point during the first appointment, you and your partner may be seen separately, perhaps when you are given a physical examination. You may then be asked if there are any skeletons in your cupboard of which your partner is ignorant, such as venereal disease, a previous conception or paternity, or an abortion, and you may be also asked more direct questions about the quality of your relationship and why you want a child. Whilst your reproductive history is obviously of some importance in terms of your infertility, you may worry that any secrets will be taken as an indication of a bad relationship. It is difficult to see how a doctor could hope to assess the quality of your relationship with your partner in a single interview. We wonder whether a doctor would refuse to offer treatment if you replied that your relationship was an unhappy one.

It is impossible to speculate on the frequency with which sexual, social or emotional problems find their way into the infertility clinic. We do believe that emotional and social factors can and do produce physical symptoms although quite how this happens is neither clear nor straightforward. However, we find objectionable the way doctors sometimes find emotional causes for infertility only when they have failed to discover a physical basis.[9] It implies that a woman who fails to conceive must be rejecting her role as mother at an unconscious level. But many women who do conceive have unwanted pregnancies and we are a long way from understanding how the two groups of women, the fertile and infertile, differ. There is no good evidence to support the idea of the emotional or psychological causation of infertility.[10] Such diagnoses are based rather on the personal judgements or hunches of doctors who have no training in the systematic assessment of your personality or of the quality of your relationship.

Questions about your sexual technique are aimed at assessing whether you have a sexual or psychological problem which prevents you from having sexual intercourse satisfactory for conception and are related to an assessment of the relationship between you and your partner. It is important to remember that infertility doctors are not trained to diagnose or treat sexual problems, or any social or emotional difficulties you may have.[11] So you need to think carefully beforehand: did you or your partner have sexual or emotional problems *before* the issue of infertility arose? If the answer is yes, then consider seriously seeking help from a specialist in psychosexual problems or try to find out about some of the self-help techniques available (the Appendix contains a booklist and details of organisations which offer help). But it is worth remembering that any sexual difficulties may have come out of your failure to conceive.

At the first appointment most doctors insist on seeing both partners. If you are not in a stable, monogamous, heterosexual relationship, then this is your first stumbling block and you may have to look elsewhere for investigations. Many women are surprised when the doctor insists on seeing their male partners because they automatically assume that they are the only ones with a problem. But there is little point in your going through all the tests without your partner's sperm being assessed.

You may find that your partner is a reluctant patient.

> I came home and I said to him, you've got to go, they won't do any more otherwise. We won't have any children if you don't. And then I burst into tears. He felt a bit guilty and said, I thought they'd sort you out without me. But he did go in the end.

You are asked for details of your medical history to discover what illnesses or operations you have had in the past for these sometimes prove important; it is well known that mumps in adulthood can seriously damage a man's testicles, or that pelvic surgery may affect a woman's Fallopian tubes. You are also asked about the type of work you do, if it involves any potentially harmful machinery or chemicals. Both you and your partner are examined physically to check that you have the characteristics normal of your sex, such as how your muscles and your hair are distributed and that your sexual organs are what they should be. For the woman, this is the first of many internal examinations. If either of you has an abnormality of the reproductive organs, it might show up here. You may both be sent for blood tests and your partner instructed to produce a semen specimen. 'We started off with the basic internal examination. Then they gave me a sterile container to take home to him for a sperm count. And then they examine you to see that you're not a funny shape, that you're quite normal.'

Finally, you should both be given a realistic assessment of the investigations, how long they might last and the chances of success.[12]

So, whilst the first appointment is relatively unobtrusive physically, it may require you to lay bare your personal life.

> I've never minded medical examinations too much. The thing I found difficult was answering the questions. At least with the examinations you can think about work or the shopping; I can

distance myself from it. But if someone asks you questions, you can't do that, you have to think up some answer.

But, this ordeal over, you can rest assured that you are unlikely to be subjected to that type of enquiry again. In fact, should you wish to talk about any sexual and emotional problems you are experiencing arising out of your infertility, it is unlikely that you will be encouraged to do so. Although sex may seem to dominate your life, it is curiously ignored by the doctor.

They've got just as many problems talking about sex as we have. When they're telling you to have intercourse, they're usually brusque. That's their defence against it being an extremely awkward subject both for them and for you. It makes us uncomfortable so I suppose it makes them uncomfortable too.

Nevertheless, you may feel the need to discuss certain problems with them, or to seek help and sympathy with certain difficulties you are having.

There's a coyness about the way they handle sex. It's as if infertility has nothing to do with sex, yet it's everything to do with it. I never know whether I want them to assume that I don't have any problems or whether I want them to ask me if I do have any difficulties.

The following appointments are taken up with tests, being given the results, each followed by another set of instructions. At some point, you may receive a firm diagnosis of your problem, or learn that some treatment has not worked. These moments are very powerful emotionally, and you may be shocked by their intensity. 'When they told me that my tubes were blocked, I wept the whole of that night. Literally, I just lay awake and sobbed. I couldn't be comforted, there was nothing anyone could do.'

Finding out that you need treatment, that something is wrong with you, can be very frightening, although it might mean the end of your worries. 'She said, you need treatment immediately. That meant there was something wrong with me. I felt deeply upset because I couldn't imagine that at the end of it I would be all right.'

Or you may find that months go by and you are no closer to discovering why you cannot conceive. Finding yourself no nearer a solution, you may wonder if it is worth continuing. 'I got the feeling that they didn't want me to come back but that they didn't want to say it. Because if I said something like, it isn't fair, he would say, well, you don't have to come back.'

We found it helpful to prepare ourselves in advance of each appointment. If you find that once in the consulting room you forget what you wanted to say, then write down your questions beforehand and take them with you. If you feel it is difficult to get the information you want because the doctor is elusive, then try to persist, or take someone with you who can ask the questions for you. This may be difficult when each visit takes several hours, much of it waiting your turn to see the doctor and then waiting for a particular test to be carried out. Not many employers welcome frequent absences from work, but there are enormous advantages to having someone with you. 'I can trust him to assimilate what is being said. He is able to take it in. And I also think that the doctor can see that we really care for each other, that it isn't just me who wants a child.'

It can be difficult for men to understand how devastating it may be to attend the clinic and they see their partner's behaviour as irrational or self-destructive. Men often find it difficult to appreciate how taking all this time off work, waiting in clinics, going through investigations and waiting day by day to see whether you are pregnant this month, can drive even the sanest woman to hysteria. Partners who themselves have attended the clinics seem to be more sensitive to this, and we feel they should be encouraged to attend. In this way, they can realise what the experience is like and behave more supportively.

> Every time I went to the hospital, I'd feel very shaky and undermined and upset that I wasn't doing it well. He was much more philosophical. Apart from the sexual side of it, he was very good about it. But he didn't really have to go and have any tests; it was me who did.

When men are expected to attend for tests, they are often less philosophical.

> He was supposed to go and have a test, which he didn't. He got all funny about it. All worried about it. When I went back, the doctor said he wouldn't do anything until my husband came in and had the test. I was annoyed with him for not going. They could have given me the container to take home, he wouldn't have minded about that. I came home and told him and he felt a bit guilty about it and said he thought they'd sort me out.

SCHEDULE OF TESTS

The schedule of tests given in Figure 4.1 is not a timetable; each clinic carries out the tests in its own way and at its own pace. Many medical textbooks suggest that the basic tests can be completed in three to five months. Based on the experiences of the women we spoke to, we think this is very optimistic.[13] Some clinics carry out a group of tests at the same time, whereas others do each test in turn and treat any problem that shows up before going on to the next test. So, for example, if your cervical mucus appears to be hostile, this is treated before your Fallopian tubes are checked. Although you may assume that you will be given a series of tests and then treated, rarely do the investigations follow such a neat plan. In fact, you may even find yourself going over the same ground that you have already covered, perhaps with different results. In some cases,

SCHEDULE OF INFERTILITY TESTS

Test	Cycle Day	Performed by
Tests on Women		
Tests of Ovulation		
Basal Body temperature	throughout	you
Blood test-progesterone level	24	laboratory
Endometrium biopsy	19	doctor; general anaesthetic
Observation of ovaries via		
laparoscopy	second half	doctor; general anaesthetic
Mucus quality		
– using post-coital	at ovulation	doctor
– observation	throughout	you or doctor
Tests of Reproductive System		
Blowing tubes	anytime	doctor
HSG	10	X-ray dept.
Laparoscopy	second half	doctor; general anaesthetic
Physical examination	anytime	doctor
Tests on Men		
Physical examination	anytime	doctor
Semen test (sperm count)	anytime	himself, processed at lab
Sperm antibody blood test	anytime	laboratory
Tests of Compatibility		
Post-coital test	at ovulation	by doctor on woman
Sperm/mucus invasion test	at ovulation	by doctor on mucus using semen sample

Figure 4.1

more than one problem is uncovered and the treatment given for the first problem turns out to be irrelevant.

I wanted them to do the tests on me at the same time as they treated him. I was worried that they'd treat him without finding out what was wrong with me. I've always had irregular periods and if there was something wrong with me, treating him would have been a waste of time.

One reason why the tests are carried out at different times is that different tests need to be done on particular days of your cycle. Figure 4.2, on the next page, shows the probable timing of some of the more commonly used tests. Other tests, including those on your partner, can be carried out at any time.

You may feel very confused by the scheduling of your tests and anxious at the length of time they take. On the other hand, your problem may be discovered very early in the investigations; although there are obvious advantages to this, delays can serve their purpose in that they allow you to adjust to your infertility.

They never actually said that there was no chance until about a

TIMING OF INFERTILITY TESTS

Day in cycle	Test
1 ⌉	1 Basal Body Temperature (BBT); throughout cycle
2	
3 Period	
4	
5 ⌋	
6	
7	
8	
9	
10	2 HSG X-ray on day 10 after period and before ovulation
11	
12	
13	
14	
15	3 Post-coital test around ovulation
16	
17	4 Laparoscopy; after ovulation
18	
19	
20	5 Endometrial biopsy; after ovulation
21	
22	
23	6 Progesterone blood test; day 20-24
24	
25	
26	
27	
28	
29	

Figure 4.2

year after I started. I had a year to come to terms with the idea that nothing would work. When they finally said that there was nothing they could do, I was depressed but not so depressed as I would have been a year earlier.

If you find the pace of your tests a problem, then try and have it changed. If the tests are going too slowly for you, speak to your doctor, ask why there are so many delays. If the reason is administrative, or because of some belief the doctor holds, then consider changing doctor; but you may find that your present doctor is sympathetic to your wish to speed up the procedure. If the tests are going too quickly for you, then try to space them out by asking for your next appointment to be delayed or by taking some time off from the investigations altogether. You may worry that you have to show a willingness to persist with any test or any treatment, and so our advice may be difficult for you to follow, but remember that the tests are for your benefit.

The tests and treatments are often discussed in ways that might be used to describe an MOT test on a car; first you check to see that all the different parts are in working order and then repair those which appear faulty. The test here is clearly separate from the treatment.[14] But for some infertility procedures, this distinction is not so clear and it is only for convenience sake that we have talked about them separately. Some tests, for example a blood test or a semen test, are clearly distinct from any treatment they indicate. But there are others where the test may also act as treatment. For instance, an X-ray of your Fallopian tubes (an HSG) shows whether your tubes are open, but it can also clear a blockage, so it works both as a test and a treatment. Then there are treatments which are also important for tests. One of these is oestrogen, which is

INFERTILITY TESTS

Test		What test is looking for	Treatment
Tests on Men			
Physical examination	(i) (ii)	descended testes varieocele	operate
Sperm count	(i) (ii)	sperm numbers motility and normality of sperm	AID depending on cause, baggy knickers, cold water spray, antibodies treatment
Blood tests	(i)	antibodies	reduce antibodies – steroids
Tests on Women			
Physical examinations	(i)	check general condition of uterus, vagina, ovaries	
Temperature chart (BBT)	(i) (ii)	ovulation intercourse at right time	stimulate ovulation give information about fertile time
Endometrial biopsy	(i) (ii)	ovulation state of uterus	stimulate ovulation increase progesterone
Post-coital test (PCT)	(i)	condition of mucus	improve quality: treat infection, douche, give oestrogen
	(ii)	sperm present and motile	advice about sexual technique, or treatments to improve sperm
	(iii)	compatibility of mucus and sperm	oestrogen to make mucus less hostile, improve sperm motility, douche
HSG	(i)	shape of uterus – double/ septum	operate, possibly
	(ii) (iii)	fibroids tubes patent	operate if necessary clear infection, surgery
Laparoscopy	(i)	condition of ovaries	operate, hormonal treatment for cysts
	(ii)	condition of tubes	clear infection, surgery
Blood tests	(i) (ii) (iii)	progesterone level prolactin level antibodies	stimulation of ovulation reduce level reduce antibodies, use sheath

Figure 4.3

sometimes given to improve the quality of mucus. It can also be given before a post-coital test carried out when you are not ovulating, to give a clearer indication of the viability of your partner's sperm in your mucus. You may become very confused and find it difficult to distinguish between a test and a treatment. Doctors sometimes blur this distinction themselves; there is even a name for it – empirical treatment. This means that a treatment is given where a cause is not clearly indicated, but if that treatment works, then the doctor reasons backwards to what your problem was.

You experience many ups and downs as you go through infertility investigations. Each new test or treatment raises your hopes, and should it fail, your disappointment may increase. Each appointment at the hospital serves as a reminder that time is passing. There are moments when we all wish to deny our infertility or our desire for a child but it is less easy to escape once you get into the routine of tests and treatments. Your infertility has truly become your focus.

BECOMING AN INFERTILITY EXPERT

Infertility is often experienced as losing control over life plans as well as over bodily functioning. A common way of dealing with feelings of helplessness is to try to take bodily control by finding out more about infertility, by reading medical textbooks. Finding out about how your body works and making sense of medical textbooks can become very absorbing and you may become known as an expert among your friends. 'I often get people ringing up and saying, what's the best day to make love if you want to get pregnant? I'm always being asked advice.'

It is also a way of ensuring that you get the most from your investigations. When you have the burden of keeping track of the course of the investigations and making sure that the right tests are done or the right drugs taken on the correct day, then knowing what lies behind the procedures can be helpful. But whilst we believe that medical knowledge is not the prerogative of doctors, it is naive to think that simply by being knowledgeable you have greater control over your investigations and treatment. The power of doctors has its source as much in their status and access to facilities as in their medical knowledge.[15] In fact, when this knowledge is subject to scrutiny, it is often found to be less firmly grounded than you might have thought. Becoming an infertility expert makes you aware of the limitations of the treatment available. We have confined ourselves to the tests and treatments most commonly used in Britain to the exclusion of the rarer types of disorders and treatments. If you are unfortunate enough to be suffering from a rare condition, or if you are receiving some esoteric or experimental treatment, the information you need will not be found in this book. We set out to highlight the *experience* of infertility because we believe that by sharing this, infertile women will feel less isolated and will find the support to improve the quality of their lives.

WHAT YOU CAN DO TO HELP YOURSELF

Sexual intercourse

The timing, frequency and position in which you have sexual intercourse can be important. Clearly, to maximise your chances of conception, you should have sexual intercourse around the time that you ovulate. One way to find out whether you are ovulating and when in your cycle it happens is to take your temperature each morning (see p. 75); another is to monitor the changes in your cervical mucus.[16] You need to try to ensure that sexual intercourse takes place just before or just around the time of ovulation so that there are plenty of live sperm inside you ready to fertilise your egg. Although it would be heartening to imagine sperm waiting around for you to ovulate, no one is very sure how long sperm can survive inside a woman's body; it probably varies quite considerably, some sperm being better survivors than others and some women's bodies providing a more welcoming environment. So it is probably good advice to have sexual intercourse every other day around the time of ovulation if that fits in with your life.

Try not to become fixated by your temperature; the basal body temperature is only a crude indicator of your menstrual cycle.

I threw my thermometer out, I couldn't stand it any longer. I worked out when I thought I would ovulate and tried to have sex around that time. It was rough and ready, but I knew by then that the thermometer was no more reliable, and it did make sex seem a little more spontaneous.

In terms of conception, it is often claimed that the best position for sexual intercourse is one where you lie on your back with your legs apart and your knees slightly bent because this position allows the penis to penetrate deeper into the vagina. A cushion may also be placed beneath your bum to raise your pelvis still further. The penis should not be withdrawn immediately after ejaculation as it may bring some of the semen out at the same time; instead, to reduce sperm loss, the penis should remain inside the vagina until it is flaccid. Lying down for a few minutes after intercourse allows the cervix to remain dipped in the pool of semen for longer. Do not use any lubricants as they can kill sperm; if you need some form of lubrication, use saliva. Do not douche (that is, introduce water into your vagina) after intercourse, although a wipe down outside should not do any harm. Where either you or your partner is overweight, or where your uterus is retroverted or tipped,[14] (your doctor should inform you of this after an internal examination), a better position for intercourse is one where you crouch and your partner enters from behind. Whilst the positions described above may increase your chances of conception, there is no clear evidence that they do work, and they are not the only ones you need employ. It is not necessary to have an orgasm to conceive; in fact, after months of having sex to order it may be a relief to discover this. What you do the rest of the month is up to you and probably does not affect conception.

Changing your lifestyle

Your lifestyle can affect your fertility, so if you or your partner are grossly over or under weight, or your diet is inadequate, or you drink, smoke or take drugs, you may be reducing your chances of conceiving. At the same time, your infertility may increase your dependence on anything which takes your mind off your anxiety and distress, so you may find it hard to give them up during investigations. Consider, though, getting your weight right and improving your diet.

There are external agents, such as chemicals and some productive processes which can reduce fertility. If you think your work or your partner's work may have something to do with your infertility, then try to find out if other men or women are also having problems. Contact the Women and Work Hazards Group for advice at the address given in the Appendix.

Alternative Therapies

So far, we have discussed western, allopathic medical treatment of infertility. We have pointed out that it cannot always uncover a problem or provide a cure. The underlying conceptual approach to allopathic medicine is to treat the body as a set of systems, each separate from the others. Your infertility tests and treatments, in theory, focus only on your reproductive system. Alternative therapies are based on different underlying conceptions of how the human body works. An alternative therapist may come to a different conclusion as to the cause of your infertility, and different diagnostic techniques are used which look at your whole body and the life you lead. To illustrate the different approaches, your hospital doctor may tell you that you are infertile because your Fallopian tubes are blocked, or because your ovaries do not produce sufficient progesterone. An alternative therapist takes these conditions to be symptoms of an underlying disorder which affects your whole body and not just your reproductive organs, and the cause of this disorder to lie outside your body in your way of life. In many respects this approach can seem more sympathetic as your childlessness is concerned with the quality of your life. Should you find that you are dissatisfied with the way your investigations are proceeding, or if you favour alternative therapies, see the contact addresses in the Appendix.

MALE INFERTILITY AND
'ARTIFICIAL INSEMINATION BY DONOR' (AID)

In this chapter, we look at infertility investigations and treatment with a discussion of the male reproductive system; the problems which can affect male fertility; tests on male fertility, especially the semen test; and some of the treatments available. We focus specifically on artificial insemination by donor.

In at least one in three cases of infertility, the cause is the poor quality of the man's semen. In men, fertility and potency (the ability to have sexual relations) are often confused. Throughout our account, we have tried to keep clear the distinction between fertility and potency.

THE MALE REPRODUCTIVE SYSTEM

The male reproductive system, like that of the female, is governed by hormones produced in the pituitary and thyroid glands, and in the testes. It is not clear exactly how these hormones act on the male reproductive organs. The male reproductive organs are illustrated in figure 5.1.

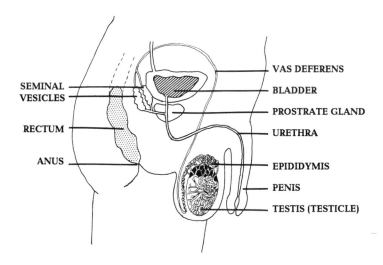

Figure 5.1. Male Reproductive System

The testes have two functions: to produce testosterone and spermato-genesis. Testosterone is the most important male hormone, responsible for the development of the characteristics we associate with a normal male, that is hair and muscle distribution and a deep voice. It also affects the metabolism and stimulates the formation of various chemicals which are necessary for the production of healthy sperm and seminal fluid, but its action is poorly understood. The production of testosterone is regulated by the pituitary gland.

The other function of the testes is spermatogenesis: the production of sperm. Sperm are produced continuously, growing from small germ cells into immature sperm. The two functions of the testes are separate so that where spermatogenesis is impaired, the production of testosterone may continue as normal. Immature sperm pass into the epididymis where they remain for some time during which they become motile, that is, able to swim. This whole process takes about seventy-two days. Prior to ejaculation, sperm leave the epididymis through the 'vas deferens'. As they pass through what are called the accessory sex organs, including the seminal vesicle and the prostate gland, the sperm are joined by the seminal fluid. Seminal fluid is alkaline, rich in nutrients which help the sperm survive and swim; it makes up the major part of the ejaculate or semen. So the ejaculate normally consists of two parts, the sperm and the seminal fluid. The semen then passes into the urethra. The urethra is connected also to the bladder, but this connection is closed when the penis is erect. The penis deposits the semen in the vagina during sexual intercourse.

The process by which sperm are produced is a long and complicated one. Sperm cells grow continuously, some reaching maturity as others are beginning to develop. Sperm are produced in vast quantities; a man may ejaculate up to three hundred million sperm at any one time. It is not clear why so many should be produced. Obviously, the sperm have a long way to travel and many get lost or destroyed on the way; probably around 200 sperm survive the journey to the Fallopian tubes. One school of thought is that although only one sperm is needed to fertilise an egg, others may be needed to assist the passage of that one and its fusion with the egg. Nor is it clear how many sperm are necessary for a man to be considered fertile; some men with few sperm father children whereas others with more fail to do so. What this suggests is that it is not simply the numbers of sperm that are important. (Another factor here is the fertility of the woman herself, and this is discussed in chapter 7.) The quality of those sperm is another factor; the production of sperm is a vast enterprise but it is not perfectly efficient. Quite a large proportion of the sperm produced are misshapen in some way. Sperm are made up of two parts: the head which contains all the genetic material and the tail which enables it to move. Some sperm have odd-shaped heads, or even two heads; others lack tails. It is quite normal for some sperm to be misshapen and abnormal in this way. It is thought to be unlikely that such abnormal sperm would get as far as an egg and fertilise it. To fertilise an egg, sperm have to be able to move. This ability, called motility, is another factor influencing fertility. Some sperm move better than others and semen containing a large proportion of immotile sperm is unlikely to be fertile.

So, in summary, for a man to be fertile, he must be able to produce an adequate number of normal, live and motile sperm, an adequate amount of seminal fluid, and he must be capable of ejaculating the semen into the woman's vagina. Infertility occurs when any one of these criteria is not met.

TESTS OF MALE INFERTILITY

Only a few tests are available so that a man's experience of infertility investigations is likely to be much shorter than a woman's. The main test used is the semen test.

The semen test

This is a very simple test. To allow sperm to build up and to maximise the chances of getting a good sample, some clinics stipulate that the man should not ejaculate for two to four days before the test. Doctors vary in the length of abstinence they require prior to the test. The sample must be collected by masturbation into a sterile container provided by the clinic and not by intercourse using coitus interruptus (withdrawal), nor by using a condom. No lubricants should be used as they can destroy the sperm. It is important to follow these instructions, to collect all the sample and not to lose any, because the total volume is measured. And because the first half of the ejaculate is richer in sperm than the second, if only a part is collected the assessment may be inaccurate. The sample should be kept warm, at body temperature, and delivered to the laboratory as soon as possible. It is important to mark on the container the time at which the specimen was produced because semen deteriorates quickly and any delay is taken into account. Many men find it hard to comply with these instructions. The problem is exacerbated because some hospital laboratories process semen only on certain days of each week so these demands have to be complied with as well.

The semen test may be repeated on a number of occasions, particularly if the first test gives a poor result. It is necessary to check whether this result is a true indication of the quality of a man's semen or whether the poor result came about because of mishandling, delays by the laboratory, or because the factors which were depressing the quality of the semen were only temporary, such as illness.

What do we learn from the semen test?:

This gives information about the numbers and proportion of motile and normal sperm present in the ejaculate and about the volume of the ejaculate. Your partner may be told the figures the laboratory produces for each of these or he may just be told how the sample is rated. Sperm numbers are given as so many million sperm per cc (cubic centimetre). Not every sperm is counted, instead a small sample is taken and counted and the numbers are rounded up. A sperm count goes from zero sperm up to a 100 million per cc and more. If your partner has no sperm, then it is clear that he is unable to make you pregnant. Some doctors consider 20 million sperm per cc is the lower limit of fertility but there is no consensus about this because it has been discovered that many men attending clinics to have vasectomies have counts well below this. These are men who have fathered children and so it has become quite clear that a figure below 20 million sperm per cc can be quite sufficient for conception. Much below that figure you are less likely to conceive but it is by no means impossible. With between 20 and 50 million sperm per cc conception is considered possible, but because there are fewer sperm, the odds are lower and it may take longer. Over 50 million per cc, sperm numbers should not present a problem.

The quality of the sperm may be more important than their number and so this is also assessed in the semen test. Results are usually given as a percentage, so 65 per cent motility means that 65 per cent of the sperm observed were motile or moving. If the sperm are to fertilise the egg, then enough of them must be moving. If 60 to 65 per cent or more of the sperm are motile, motility is not a problem. If less than half of the sperm are motile, then their sluggishness makes it more difficult for you to conceive. This is all guesswork really, especially when what is being measured is the sperm's ability to move around some hours after they have been ejaculated and after having been stored in a sterile container. Under these conditions, the sperm become sluggish quite quickly so it is clearly important to do the test soon after ejaculation and to ensure that the sample is kept at body temperature. If the test is done two hours after ejaculation then there are fewer immotile sperm than if the test were performed later.

Of course, during sexual intercourse the sperm are deposited inside the woman's vagina and not into a sterile container. Many of them are soon found in the cervix where the woman's body provides a more welcoming environment. So the fact that many of the sperm are unable to swim after sitting on the laboratory shelf for several hours does not mean that the same proportion of them would be immotile inside a woman's body after that length of time. A more serious condition is agglutination where the sperm lie huddled together, unable to move. This is due to the presence of antibodies.

The numbers of abnormal sperm in a semen test are also given as a percentage so that a figure of 65 per cent here means that 65 per cent of the sperm are normally shaped and that 35 per cent are abnormal and therefore unlikely to be able to fertilise an egg. A high proportion of abnormal sperm means that a woman may have problems in conceiving. It is interesting how sperm are talked about in terms of their motility and normality whereas discussion of women's problems is peppered with negative terms such as hostility, incompetence and suchlike.

These three measures (count, morphology and motility) are closely associated with one another so a low sperm count is often accompanied by a high proportion of immotile and abnormally shaped sperm. But it is possible to have a high sperm count and many dead or abnormal sperm or a low sperm count with a high proportion of normal, motile sperm.

The laboratory also measures the volume of the ejaculate. Between three and five cc of ejaculate is considered normal. Quantities above or below this are more likely to be associated with other abnormalities of the semen. When the semen is first ejaculated, it is a liquid. This liquid quickly forms a gel which returns to a liquid after about twenty minutes. This change probably has some significance for the sperm's survival as well as perhaps maximising its chances of being retained in the vagina. But this is all guesswork. If the semen is too liquid or too thick, it presents a fertility problem.

The semen test is an easy one to do and it gives some information about the quality of a man's semen. If the sperm count and the other measures suggest that the semen is of good quality, then your partner is probably not the major cause of your infertility. If the sperm count is zero, it is clear that you will never get pregnant by this man and that you have to think about other ways of getting pregnant, such as artificial insemination using donor semen, or about adoption. However, if the semen is rated below average, then the position is less clear cut. The semen test should be repeated to make sure that the ratings are consistent and not just freak results. But if the same result is obtained again, then other tests of the semen, especially the post-coital test, are usually carried out. A semen test somewhere between very poor and reasonably good tells you that it may be possible to conceive by this man; it cannot tell you much more than this, partly because the information is not there, and partly because how successful these sperm are depends considerably on the woman's body. All the test can do is give you some indication of the odds.

They didn't say it's totally impossible because everybody knows of men with low fertility who get their women pregnant. They just said that our chances were so remote that it wasn't worth holding out any hope. You can't keep trying every month hoping this time we'd do it.

You then have to decide whether these are odds that you can plan around or can pin your hopes on. You may be prepared to wait and see, hoping that one day you might be lucky.

Lots of people do the football pools, but they don't organise their finances on the million-to-one chance that they'll win. I don't see why I should do that about having kids. You'd say I was stupid if I did that with my finances, why are kids any different?

The semen test, as the main test of male fertility, is usually one of the first tests given. But in some hospitals, it comes after a number of tests have been carried out on the woman. 'I've had the HSG and I'm still waiting for the results of that. And I've had a post-coital test. They found something not quite right there so now he has to have a semen test.'

It is clearly important to check the man's semen early in the investigations before the woman has tests unnecessarily. However, some men refuse to have the test and some women may not be in a relationship where they feel that they can or want to ask their partner to have a test. We feel that a woman should still be able to be investigated even where the semen test will not form part of the investigation.

You may be surprised when a semen test is carried out at an early stage of the investigations. We all have strong ideas about infertility being a woman's problem and it can come as a shock to have doubts about a man's fertility raised. You may feel that whilst you are ready to start the infertility investigations and are willing to go for tests, your partner may not yet have reached that point. He may not be ready to put his fertility on the line, to have it tested, and until he is ready to do so, you may feel that you have no option but to delay the semen test.

Other tests of male infertility

There are a number of other tests of male infertility which supplement the information obtained from the semen test. One is the physical examination. Many clinics insist that both men and women attend the first appointment and it is on this occasion that a physical examination is often carried out. The purpose of this is to discover any abnormalities, such as a varicocele (a varicose vein in one or both testes). Some men develop varicocele at puberty, others later, perhaps after fathering children. A varicocele is thought to affect fertility by reducing the numbers and quality of the sperm although it is not clear why this should happen. One idea is that the extra blood pressure in the testes raises the temperature and so destroys many of the sperm. Certainly, sperm do not like heat and survive best at a temperature a degree or two lower than body temperature, which is why the testes hang outside the body.

At the physical examination, a man's general health and development is looked at. Distribution of hair and other secondary sexual characteristics may give clues as to whether hormones are produced in sufficient quantities. He is also asked when his testes descended, whether he has had mumps or venereal disease, whether he is taking drugs, smokes or drinks heavily and the sort of work he does, all of which can provide some clues about possible causes of infertility.

Although clearly this is information which can easily be obtained at a first appointment, in only a few cases is it likely to be useful. Another test of male fertility is the post-coital test (described in chapter 7) to examine the sperm inside the woman's body, to look at the quantity and quality and to see how well they survive. Knowing how the sperm survive in this environment may give some clues about factors which may be interfering with the sperm's effectiveness. Very occasionally, other tests may be tried, such as a testicular biopsy, where a small piece of tissue is removed from the testes. This may tell whether sperm are being produced or whether the problem may be located in one of the other sexual organs. Blood tests are sometimes carried out either to measure the level of testosterone or to look for sperm antibodies.

You can see that the number of tests available to measure a man's fertility is not very extensive, far fewer than are available for women. A man's experience of infertility investigations, whatever the outcome, is short-lived.

Getting the results of tests
Waiting for the results of infertility tests is an anxious experience.

> When the results came through, he breathed a sigh of relief. It was
> only then that I realised how anxious he was. They said he had a
> high sperm count which made him very happy. They may have
> eliminated him, but it doesn't seem to have got us anywhere.

Finding out that your partner has poor semen comes as a blow. Doctors
find it very hard to deliver bad news.

> She said, 'Your husband has . . .', she started to say a very low sperm
> count and sort of choked and said, 'it's a bit low.' I looked at her
> and I thought, she's not telling me the truth. What she means is
> there are hardly any there. She wasn't honest about it.

Sometimes bad news is confused with the way it is given; there is no way
that bad news can be given which prevents it coming as a shock, so
blaming the doctor cannot help. Because men so rarely attend the
infertility clinics, the woman may be the one who has to bring the bad
news home to her partner. This is not an easy thing to do.

> I went straight over to my friend. I kept saying, what am I going
> to say. I don't want to be the one who has to tell him. I don't want
> to hurt him.

You may find that a way round this problem is to take your partner with
you to see the doctor when you know that the results of his semen test
will be available. If the result is poor, you are relieved of the
responsibility of breaking the news to your partner, and instead of him
being angry with you, you can share the shock and sadness together.
Your partner also has the opportunity to ask any questions he may have
about the result as well as undergoing any further tests, such as a
physical examination or blood tests.
    The difficulty with a poor result of a semen test is that inevitably it
assigns the responsibility of your childlessness to your partner. You may
feel very angry with him for denying you the possibility of having a
child; and you may feel sad that you will be unable to bear his child,
perhaps because of particular qualities in him which you hoped to see
in your child. Here you are, as far as you know, capable of conceiving
and bearing a child, but with a partner unable to fulfil his role. At the
same time, your partner is living through his own loss of fertility, perhaps
spreading this sense of failure into other areas of his life. No doubt, you
feel sympathy for him, and this conflicts with your anger.
    You may even feel that you would prefer the infertility to have been
your problem; dealing with the inevitable tensions between you and
your partner can seem too difficult.

> I'd prefer it if it was the other way round. He's so upset and finds

it very difficult to cope with. Men don't talk to each other about their problems. He's got no one to talk to about it.

The difficulties are there but we feel that you should be able to rejoice in your own fertility whilst feeling sympathy for your partner. Remember that you can still become a mother, although this might seem too difficult to contemplate at the moment. You may be surprised to find how time softens the blow for both of you, and how solutions which you would never dream of considering become feasible and attractive options.

When I look back over how I felt, at my anger with him and at how much I blamed him, and how I refused even to consider any alternatives, I am astonished to see how much I have changed and to find myself contemplating steps which not that long ago I had dismissed as impossible.

We are not trying to underestimate the tensions such a situation creates but we feel that it is important to recognise that you and your partner are two separate individuals. Whilst infertility is the problem you both face, that does not mean that you experience it in the same way: you are concerned with your own childlessness whilst your partner is addressing himself to his damaged self-image. By recognising these tensions and coming to terms with them, you may reach a solution which is acceptable to you both.

MALE INFERTILITY AND MASCULINITY

The investigation and treatment of male infertility is considered by doctors to be a very delicate procedure, one to be carried out with great sensitivity.

When we went to the clinic, the doctor said, 'I don't want to worry you and I don't want you to think any the less of yourself, but we do consider your sperm count is slightly below average.' The way he said it made me think that he didn't know what to say, but also that he was telling us the way he would feel if that were him.

This is because we usually think of men's masculinity, their ability to have sexual relations and their fertility as being linked. So it is assumed that a man who has a very active sex life, or that a tough, chunky man, must be more fertile than a weak, skinny man. There is a level at which this linking operates. If a man cannot maintain an erection or deposit his semen in a woman's vagina then he is quite unlikely to father children. In this sense potency is necessary for fertility, but the opposite is not true. A man may be sexually active, able to maintain an erection, to ejaculate and able to give pleasure to a woman but still be infertile. And a man who is not sexually active may have a good sperm count and be able easily to father children. Problems in these two areas often have quite different causes. Poor results of a semen test are likely to have a physical cause whereas impotence is often a symptom of psychosexual difficulties and can only rarely be traced to a physical cause. If a man thinks his problems are psychosexual, the best course is to seek a remedy specifically for psychosexual problems; infertility doctors are trained in the medical aspects of reproduction and are not qualified either to diagnose or to treat psychosexual problems.

But knowing that potency, fertility and masculinity are not connected in this way may not make you or your partner more relaxed about having to go through the tests nor make it easier to cope with the blow to his self-esteem if his fertility is in doubt. In some cases, the investigations themselves can lead to psychosexual problems.

It took months for our sex life to get back to what it was before we found out he was infertile. I suppose he was rather unhappy and I felt strange about all those funny sperm in my vagina.

THE CAUSES OF MALE INFERTILITY

We have little information about how or why a man has a poor sperm count.[2] Indeed, we have far less information about men than we have about women and their problems. There have been very few attempts to interfere with male fertility. Consequently we remain very ignorant about how the male reproductive system works and what can go wrong, and so little is available in the way of tests or treatment.

The tests of male fertility focus on sperm and its production. Tests of men's hormone levels and an examination of the functioning of the various parts of the man's reproductive system are not part of most men's infertility investigations in the way that they are for women. Instead, by examining the semen an attempt is made to locate where the problem lies, more often than not by guesswork. But because there are so many processes involved in the development of sperm, knowing that a man has a low sperm count may not enable the doctor to establish with any degree of accuracy why this condition arose.

Unlike their approach to women, when there is no known reason for men's infertility, doctors rarely use psychological factors as an explanation. This might be because they take refuge in accepting the limitations of their knowledge about male reproduction or because they are more reticent about acknowledging men's psychological problems. We have come across no discussions by doctors about men being infertile because they are rejecting their masculinity.[3]

Like female infertility, male infertility can remain hidden for a long time. It is only when a man wants a child that he may discover that he is infertile, perhaps years after his fertility was impaired. Trying to find out more about this means hunting around in people's pasts or keeping vast registers of people exposed to particular hazards.

Some factors associated with male infertility have short-term effects on fertility whereas other factors have a permanent effect. Congenital conditions, injury or illnesses such as mumps, can lead to permanent sterility; testes which do not descend into the scrotum until adolescence may never produce live sperm. The testicles are very vulnerable to damage as they lie unprotected outside the man's body, and the increasing number of environmental hazards may account for the growing incidence of male infertility. These hazards destroy the germ cells from which the sperm develop, leaving no chance of the testicles ever producing sperm again. A number of factors, however, may temporarily depress sperm production or their motility without destroying the ability of the testes to produce sperm. These include heat, illness, overwork, tiredness, drugs and alcohol; also men who do certain kinds of jobs, such as driving lorries or working in very hot conditions, may have more short-term fertility problems.

TREATMENT OF MALE INFERTILITY

The treatment used in male infertility takes one of two forms: the first tries to improve the quality of the sperm; the second involves bypassing the poor quality semen and using instead the semen of another man – artificial insemination using donor semen (AID).

If a man is azoospermic, that is, he produces no sperm at all, then the tests may give some information about the cause, but there is nothing available in the way of treatment. For research purposes, or perhaps because he is an interesting case, further tests may be carried out. Some men are curious to know why they are infertile and want to explore the causes even where they know that this will not lead to treatment. Others may prefer to put their energies into thinking about artificial insemination using donor semen.

If a man is oligospermic, that is, produces few sperm, little can be done to increase their numbers but there are different techniques for trying to improve their effectiveness. One such technique is artificial insemination using your partner's semen. For this, your partner has to masturbate and his semen is sometimes treated before it is placed inside you. The semen is deposited either high in your vagina or at the entrance to the cervix. Artificial insemination may also be used if your partner produces too much seminal fluid or if his seminal fluid is too watery or too thick. If a sufficient number of his sperm are normal, then the split-ejaculate technique may be tried. The first portion of the ejaculate is often argued to be rich in sperm; these sperm are often more motile than those in the second part which some doctors believe contains substances harmful to sperm. The idea is to collect the first portion of the ejaculate separately from the rest so your partner may be given two containers in which to collect his semen. The first portion of the semen is then used in artificial insemination.

You may be offered a version of artificial insemination to carry out at home using an insemination cap. This is a small rubber cap which you put over the cervix and which has a long tube with a valve which hangs outside your vagina. While you insert the cap, your partner masturbates into a container. You then draw up his semen into a syringe and inject it through the tube and close the valve. The semen is then held in place against your cervix by the cap, so hopefully the sperm have nowhere to go but through the cervix into the uterus. This procedure is fiddly and it is hardly erotic but it may work for some people.

It is clearly important for any insemination technique to be used at your fertile time, thus ensuring the greatest chance of success. So you may be asked to take your temperature to try and assess when you are likely to ovulate. If these techniques are going to work, they should do so in the first three to six cycles. After that your chances of conceiving are about the same as without insemination techniques, probably because something else is damaging the sperm. You may find these techniques difficult or you may be prepared to go on trying them for some time. It is up to you to decide how much you can take and when you want to give up.

If your partner has a varicocele, then an operation can increase significantly sperm motility. This operation is one of the few treatments available for men and it roughly doubles your chances of getting pregnant. Varicocele accounts for only a small number of cases of male infertility but because the treatment can be effective, it is well worth looking into. Very occasionally, blockages in the epididymis or in the vas deferens are diagnosed and operated on but the success rate here is low.

Where hormonal imbalance may be the cause of infertility, various drug treatments have been tried such as clomiphene, bromocriptine, mesterolone, testosterone and HCG. There is no good evidence that any of these work and they are offered on an empirical, try it and see basis.[4] We feel that this should be made clear to you and that you should be told that the chances of success with these methods are not high so you can decide for yourselves whether you are prepared to try them. You may be lucky and just hit on one which works for you or you may spend months getting nowhere.

> I was on the tablets for about a year, three months on and three months off, waiting for what they called a booster to happen. We knew that she couldn't get pregnant whilst I was taking the tablets. Anyway, just as everyone had given up hope that they would work, we found out that she was pregnant.

It takes about 72 days for the testes to produce mature sperm, so the effects of any of these treatments are not seen for at least ten weeks.

If your partner's sperm agglutinate – that is gather together in clusters unable to move – then the cause may be sperm antibodies. This can be confirmed by a blood test. How these antibodies develop can only be surmised, but they are quite common in men who have had their vasectomies reversed. Some experimental treatments are being tried, such as large doses of steroids or washing the sperm to remove the antibodies, but as yet the success rate is low. This is an area in which immunologists are conducting a lot of research so it might soon be possible to treat sperm antibodies successfully.

Lastly, you may be offered treatment which owes more to the skill of the manufacturers of underwear than to any drug company or surgeon, that is, your partner may be advised to wear boxer shorts. He may also

67

be asked to spray his testicles daily with cold water. The idea is to lower the temperature of the testes slightly and so improve sperm motility. There is no evidence that these measures bring any improvement but you may feel that it is worth trying. It may at least give you both the feeling that he is doing all he can.

We were given advice about baggy pants and cold water. I thought it was hilarious but they were serious. I went out and bought him the boxer shorts but I don't think he tried the freezing water, he couldn't bring himself to do it.

If problems with your partner's semen appear to be the cause of your infertility, there is unfortunately no wonder cure available. Some of the techniques described here may help to improve poor semen quality but none of them are associated with very high success rates. Your partner may want to try them out before he is prepared to consider alternatives, but if you want to continue to try to get pregnant, your options are to trust to luck and do nothing or to think about artificial insemination using donor semen.

ARTIFICIAL INSEMINATION USING DONOR SEMEN (AID)

AID is physically a very straightforward procedure: sperm donated by a man through masturbation is taken up into a syringe and inserted into your vagina around the cervix. You then lie on your back with your knees bent for half an hour or so to give the sperm a good chance to get inside your uterus.

Donors are chosen who have a good sperm count. You are matched for general colouring of yourself and your partner and frequently for blood group. The idea is to increase your chances of having a child who looks quite like you. However, genes are not controlled so easily, as a look at the children of any parent demonstrates. Apart from this, no attempt is made to match your donor in any other ways. Like any prospective parent, you have to take genetic pot luck. You are given no information about the donor, but doctors sometimes claim that people find it reassuring to know that many donors are medical students.

Often, the semen is frozen and kept in a sperm bank until it is needed. Considerable care is taken to maintain the sperm's motility; it has to be kept in a special solution and frozen and unfrozen gently. Freezing semen is the only aspect of AID which requires technical expertise and special facilities.[5] Sometimes fresh semen is used, in which case, the man masturbates and the semen is put into your vagina soon afterwards. Sperm begin to deteriorate quite quickly so the semen has to be used within an hour or two. Where fresh semen is used, the technicalities are minimal. With both fresh and frozen semen, the main concern is to ensure that sperm are available at the right time, that is, during your fertile period. But, the procedures and the experience are the same whether fresh or newly unfrozen semen is used. Some doctors argue that fresh semen has a greater chance of making you pregnant, but much depends on how the semen is unfrozen and how long it has been hanging round the clinic before you receive it. The advantage of frozen semen is that it makes it easier to run an efficient AID service because the clinic is always sure of having some available at the right time for you.[6]

The key to the success of AID is timing, of using the semen at your most fertile point. You are advised to monitor your cycle carefully, perhaps by recording your basal body temperature. You may be given ovulation-inducing drugs to make your ovulation more predictable. Often women are inseminated twice each cycle around the time of ovulation, with a day or two between each insemination.

Between five and seven out of ten women who are given AID conceive and most conceptions take place within three to four cycles. This compares favourably with conception rates of 'normal' intercourse. Some clinics insist that you go through infertility investigations before they offer AID; others go ahead after a number of poor semen tests and start to investigate you only if you are not pregnant after three or four cycles.

If you do conceive through AID, your pregnancy is no different to that of most women, although like many infertile women you may be more aware of any risks in pregnancy and childbirth and, because of the effort in conceiving, you may worry about miscarrying. (We discuss these concerns more fully in chapter 9.) You may be anxious that using sperm that have been frozen – or even the process of AID itself – may affect the foetus. These anxieties are quite understandable, but there is no evidence that AID babies have any more problems than other babies.

How to obtain AID

AID is not a service which is freely available within the NHS. Usually, it is offered only to women whose partners have no sperm at all or only very few sperm or whose semen is of poor quality. So if your partner's semen is poor to average, you are not offered AID although no other treatment is available. Your doctor may initiate a discussion of AID or may wait for you to bring the subject up.

I've thought about AID and I would be quite happy to have it if they suggested it. But I can't ask for it myself, I feel that she'd just laugh at me if I did, she's so unsympathetic.

Non-medical criteria are also used in deciding who is to receive AID; many clinics are anxious to ensure that only people *they* consider fit for parenthood should have it, so you and your partner are questioned about your personal circumstances in a number of interviews. Those considered most fit for AID-parenthood by NHS clinics are married couples whose marriage is evaluated as stable. So if you are single or a lesbian or your marriage is judged as unstable, then you may be refused.

If you are accepted by the NHS, you may have a long wait ahead of you, up to eighteen months. There are only five NHS sperm banks, in London, Cardiff, Manchester, Sheffield and Birmingham so you may have to travel some distance for AID. Sperm die off rapidly once they are unfrozen so it is not feasible for the sperm to be sent to you.

If you do not fit the medical or social categories and so are refused AID by the NHS, there are a number of other sources. Sometimes, but not always, different standards operate in private practice but you must be prepared to pay. A more sympathetic source is the British Pregnancy Advisory Service (BPAS) who run an AID service and are willing to consider single heterosexual or lesbian women. The BPAS have several centres throughout England and you can contact them through the address in the appendix. It is a charity and charges for its services. Of course, you may consider a fleeting relationship with other men in the hope that you become pregnant. Besides the emotional problems there are practical considerations. By now, you are aware that conception may not be as easy as we are led to believe and you may not succeed in getting pregnant quickly this way.

Some women arrange their own artificial insemination, bypassing the medical system altogether through self-insemination. They ask a sympathetic man or a group of men to donate their semen and use it to inseminate themselves around ovulation. The procedure is straightforward and is discussed very sympathetically in the pamphlet 'Self Insemination'.[7]

Thinking about AID

If you choose AID because of your partner's infertility, inevitably you have to negotiate tensions and anxieties. You may readily accept AID as a solution or it may take months or years before you are prepared to consider it. But your timetable may not be the same as his. You may prefer to wait until you feel secure in his co-operation or you may feel a sense of urgency, perhaps because of your age, and go ahead with AID hoping that he comes round after the baby is born. It can seem as though you are being pulled in very different directions at once.

> If I decide to have a child and he says, no, in the end I would go ahead and do what I wanted because it's my life. I do feel ambivalent and I want to know what he feels. What worries me is that if I want a child so badly that I'm prepared to sacrifice my relationship to have one, what does that mean?'

Choosing to have AID can be difficult not only because the impression we are given is that it is slightly sordid, something to keep secret, but also because it means that you have to deal with your partner's fears and insecurities about his identity and sexuality. Women are not taught to assert themselves within their relationships, but rather to sacrifice their own preferences to nurture others. Choosing AID may mean that you have to declare what you want and hope to persuade your partner to go along with you.

> When I say I'm going to have AID whether he likes it or not, I shock people because what I am saying is that I'm putting myself first before this man and this relationship.

Of course, some men readily accept the idea of AID, realising that it represents their only chance for fatherhood.

You may find little help for the emotional difficulties you have to grapple with; most discussion of AID focuses on its legality and specifically on the legal relationship between child and father.[8]

> I asked her if there was any emotional counselling. She said, had I been told about the legal aspects. I said no, and repeated my question. She said, well, the legal side is very important. I said, I'm sure it is, but I can't change the law. I don't call that counselling, I call that giving information.

So the question which is seen to be really important is who is the child's father, its biological father (the donor) or its social father (your partner). As the law stands, an AID child is illegitimate and should be legally adopted by its social father. The issue arises when filling out the birth certificate: giving false information is strictly perjury. Because the law lays greater stress on biological rather than on social fatherhood, many women and their partners using AID are advised to keep quiet about it. But this encourages the silence about male infertility and adds to the impression that AID is underhand or sordid. By restricting itself to the legal aspects, AID counselling provides little support for women and men's feelings about AID. Both need to be able to discuss more openly their attitudes to it.

Stepfathers through adoption as well as those who accept the children of their partners, point to the positive nature of the social relationship of fatherhood. A child which is not of your genes can still be a child you can love and enjoy. In contrast, biological fatherhood in no way guarantees that a child is liked, loved or even acknowledged. So you can see that the social and biological aspects of fatherhood are not inextricably linked; instead, what is important is the quality of the relationship.

Accepting AID means giving up romantic and powerful notions about a child as the fusion of two selves.

> I've got to sort out, make it clear in my own mind, that the emotional and physical means of getting pregnant are two separate things. If you have to get sperm and an egg together, it makes no difference how you manage it, it's a separate issue to the emotional problem.

If being pregnant and giving birth is important to you, AID can be a good step to take because it enables you to have these experiences. Your partner can share your pregnancy and childbirth with you so that, except for conception, the relationship your partner has with the child is very much like that of other fathers. The circumstances of the child's conception may fade rapidly in the experience.

> He felt the child kicking inside me and he watched her being born.

71

I saw all the joy and pride of fatherhood as he held his daughter and my worries about him disappeared.

You may worry that AID may damage your relationship with your child. Should you explain the circumstances of his or her conception? Thirty years ago adoption was considered a stigma and parents were advised not to discuss it openly with their children. Perhaps anxieties about AID would similarly disappear if there were more open discussion about it. But there can never be guarantees in relationships, including that between any parent and child.

AID may appear to be a difficult route to negotiate but we believe that once you have conceived and given birth, the problems and anxieties associated with it are soon forgotten in the day-to-day business of child-rearing.

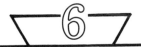

INFERTILITY IN WOMEN:
PROBLEMS IN CONCEIVING

To become pregnant you must produce an egg; this egg must be able to travel down the Fallopian tubes, and when fertilised, to implant in the uterus. If any one or more of these does not happen, or does not happen very efficiently, then you will have problems in conceiving. In this chapter we discuss first the hormonal changes that govern your menstrual cycle and ovulation and then your reproductive organs. We look at some of the disorders that can affect fertility, their investigation and the treatments available, focusing on what it feels like to go through them.

HORMONES, MENSTRUAL CYCLE AND OVULATION

Menstrual cycles are regulated by hormones which function as chemical messengers carrying instructions round the body. The hormones involved in the menstrual cycle are oestrogen, progesterone, luteinising hormone (LH) and follicle stimulating hormone (FSH). A cycle starts on the first day of your period, known as Day 1. During the early part of the cycle the ovaries, stimulated by the hypothalamus and the pituitary gland in the brain, produce oestrogen. This builds up to a maximum level in the middle of the cycle. Oestrogen stimulates the growth of the egg cell (follicle) in the ovary and of the endometrium, the lining of the uterus and also changes the quality of the cervical mucus, from thick and opaque to watery and clear, making it easier for sperm to move through.

The level of oestrogen increases towards mid-cycle which stimulates the pituitary gland to produce a massive amount of LH, known as the LH surge. LH stimulates a rapid growth of the egg (ovum) which ruptures and breaks away from its follicle in the ovary 24 hours later; this rupturing is called ovulation. You may feel a cramp at ovulation known as *mittelschmerz* (middle pain – as it occurs in the middle of the cycle).

After ovulation the follicle in which the egg developed, now without the egg, and called the 'corpus luteum' (yellow body) secretes progesterone. Progesterone increases the build up of the endometrium, ensuring that the uterus is ready to receive a fertilised egg. If 10 to 12 days after ovulation an egg is not implanted in the uterine lining then the corpus luteum begins to disintegrate and the level of progesterone falls. Without a high level of progesterone the rich uterine lining cannot be maintained. The endometrium, therefore, begins to

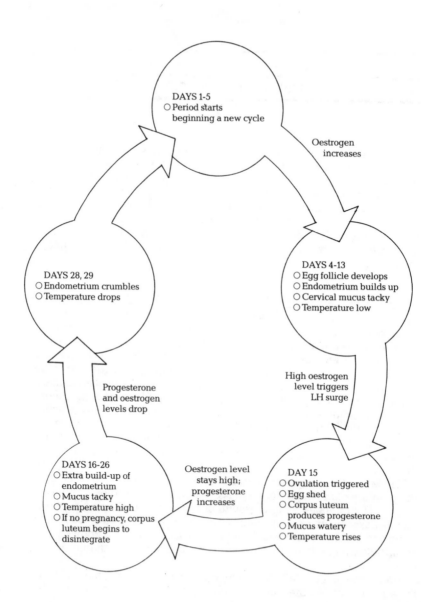

Figure 6.1. Non-pregnant menstrual cycle (29 day cycle)

crumble and is shed at menstruation, marking the beginning of the next cycle. These changes are shown in Figure 6.1.

The time from ovulation to the beginning of menstruation (the luteal phase) is about 12 to 14 days. This part of the cycle is relatively fixed, whereas the first part is more variable. So if your cycle is 30 days long, the first part, up to ovulation, is 16 to 18 days long and the second part, from ovulation to menstruation, is 12 to 14 days. If your cycle is 32 days long, the first part is 18 to 20 days long and the second part is 12 to 14 days again. But some fertile women have cycles which hardly conform to this pattern at all.

If you conceive, then the corpus luteum does not die off 10 to 12 days after ovulation; instead it is maintained by the hormone human chorionic gonadotropin (HCG) produced by the developing fertilised egg. HCG can be isolated in urine and measured as a test of pregnancy. The corpus luteum continues to produce progesterone into the early weeks of pregnancy. These changes are shown in Figure 6.2.

Hormone cycles and infertility

One of the first investigations of infertility looks at whether you are producing the right amount of each hormone and especially whether you are ovulating. Ovulation is accompanied by a whole series of hormonal and physical changes and these can be monitored to test whether ovulation has taken place; so the different infertility tests focus on these changes and measure them.

Much of the information we have about hormonal changes in the menstrual cycle, about ovulation and about the ways of inducing ovulation comes from research into contraception. More recently the development of 'in vitro' fertilisation, where the egg is fertilised outside the body, has lead to research into more accurate methods of predicting ovulation. These same changes associated with ovulation are also of interest to women using natural or rhythm methods of birth control who are keen to predict ovulation in order to prevent conception.[1]

TESTS OF OVULATION

Clearly, if you are pregnant then you must have ovulated. If you are menstruating regularly and experience some cramping, then you are probably ovulating; if you do not have periods you are very unlikely to be ovulating, but it is possible to have periods and not ovulate, for instance the periods of women using the contraceptive pill are periods at the end of non-ovulatory cycles. There are several tests for ovulation, the most widely used is the basal body temperature (BBT).

Basal body temperature (BBT)

One effect of progesterone is to make your body temperature rise slightly. More progesterone is produced in the second half of your cycle, so your temperature is lower in the first half, rising soon after ovulation with the production of progesterone by the corpus luteum, and remaining higher during the second part of your cycle. The production

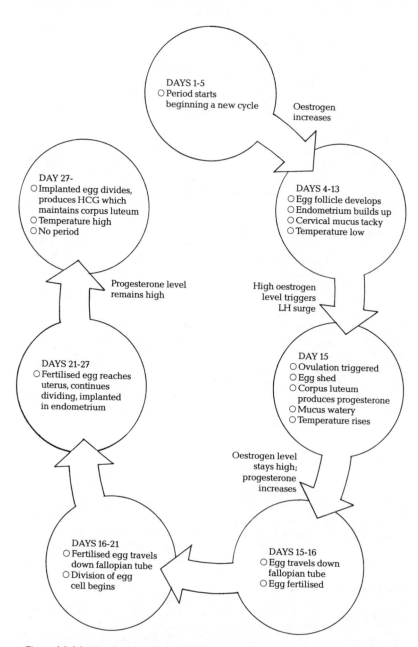

Figure 6.2. Menstrual cycle with pregnancy

of progesterone drops just before your period starts, so your body temperature also drops. If you are pregnant the progesterone level continues high, and your temperature stays at the higher level. This can be one of the first signs of pregnancy. By taking your temperature every day throughout your cycle, you can monitor these changes.

The rise in temperature is usually not very great; a difference of about 0.5°C is quite common. Your body temperature will probably vary by more than this during the course of a day, so if you want to compare your temperature on different days, it is important to make sure that you take it under the same conditions each day. The easiest way to do this is to take it first thing in the morning as soon as you wake up, before you get up, have a cup of tea or go to the loo. This temperature is called basal body and refers to the heat of the body at rest. Having a cup of tea makes your mouth warmer and getting up sets your body in motion and so raises your temperature. To be sure that you are getting a good reading you need to keep the thermometer in your mouth and under your tongue for at least two minutes, because the mercury in the thermometer takes some time to rise. If you take it out too quickly you will get a reading that is too low.

When you take the thermometer out you have to read it. You may find this a bit difficult first thing in the morning so it might be helpful to use a special fertility thermometer which has the relevant part of the scale enlarged. Once you have read your temperature, make a note of it. You then have to shake down the mercury in the thermometer, ready for use the next day. If you find it really impossible to read your thermometer first thing in the morning you can leave it, without shaking it down, to read later in the day.

Special temperature charts are available from infertility clinics and sometimes from family planning clinics. Each day you mark a dot on the chart and then you join up the dots. Your thermometer gives the temperature in degrees Fahrenheit (F) or centigrade (C). The chart probably has both scales marked. It is possible to convert from one scale to another, but as the differences in temperature which you are noting are small, you may confuse the picture by working in both scales.

Start each new cycle on a new chart. So the first day of your period is day 1 of your cycle. Then continue until the first day of your next period which will be day 1 of the next cycle. If your period stops and starts, count the first day you menstruated as day 1 and ignore the interruption. We show a number of BBT charts in figure 6.3.

The BBT is a painless test and involves a minimum of interference with your body. It is a test you can do yourself and one which it is well worth trying out for several months before going along to an infertility clinic. It provides you with information and you can take your charts along with you, perhaps thereby saving time. You may find it tedious taking your temperature every day, especially after months or perhaps years.

I broke two thermometers and I don't think it was an accident. I've stopped taking my temperature. I got to loathe waking up in the morning and reaching out for the thermometer so I stopped it.

The experience of infertility

Because you are monitoring your body carefully, you may become even more aware of where you are in your cycle, and the ups and downs in your mood may become more extreme.

Figure 6.3

Temperature Chart 1

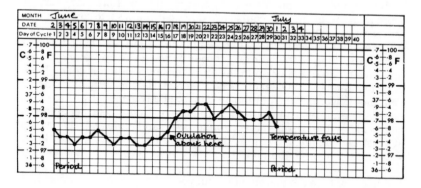

In chart 1 the woman ovulates on about day 16 and then her temperature rises. It falls on day 30, and her period starts on that day.

Temperature Chart 2

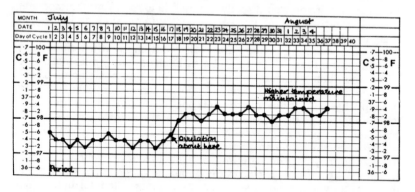

In chart 2 the woman ovulates on about day 16, her temperature rises and stays high, giving her the first indication that she is pregnant.

78

Temperature Chart 3

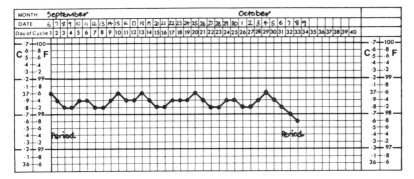

In chart 3 the temperature shows no rise in the second part of the cycle, indicating that she did not ovulate.

Temperature Chart 4

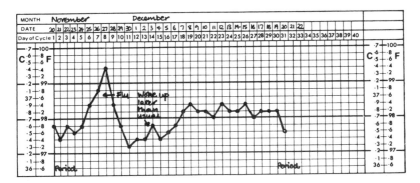

In chart 4 the woman ovulates and her temperature rises, falling again just before her period on day 31. On this chart you can see how having flue and taking her temperature much later than usual gave her a high BBT reading on those days.

What the BBT tells you: Many books on the BBT give idealised charts showing a lower temperature in the first half of the cycle, followed by a higher temperature in the second part. Your own chart may or may not follow this classic pattern, and you may find it difficult to interpret. A number of factors can affect your temperature: illness, drinking too much the night before, drugs, waking up earlier or later than usual.[2]

Your mid-cycle rise in temperature may be sharp, as in the classic diagrams, or it may rise slowly over a number of days. If the rise is slow, it is more difficult to decide exactly when you ovulated. There are large variations in temperature charts, from woman to woman, and from month to month in the same woman. We include a number of charts to give you

79

an impression of such variability, and to show how things like illness can make the pattern more difficult to interpret.

If you are not ovulating then your temperature does not show this rise in the second part of the cycle. Instead it stays very much the same throughout the cycle. (See figure 6.3, example 3.)

If you take your temperature for a number of months, making a chart for each cycle, you can see whether you are ovulating regularly. Sometimes you are asked to keep your temperature chart to monitor the effectiveness of a particular treatment.

The BBT and sexual intercourse: In chapter 4 we explain how tests can sometimes become treatment. This is true for the BBT which can be used to pinpoint ovulation so you can time intercourse to coincide with ovulation. This can be very helpful if you are not sure when you ovulate. But knowing when you ovulate can put you under pressure to regulate intercourse around your temperature chart. This pressure may be increased still further if the clinic asks you to mark an arrow on the chart each time you have intercourse. You may feel this is an embarrassing intrusion into your life, and find yourself adding or subtracting arrows to the charts to make them look more like what you think the clinic expects. In these cases, of course, the information is valueless.

> I was told to mark the charts, and was reminded a couple of times.
> I said I know roughly when we are supposed to have sex. I didn't want them to have that information. I wanted to maintain some privacy.

You may feel that your temperature chart looks very scientific and so must be an accurate guide to ovulation and to when you should have intercourse. But there is a lot of disagreement about how the charts should be interpreted. It is the LH surge which triggers ovulation, but it is the rise in progesterone after ovulation that brings about the rise in temperature. It is not clear just how long it takes the corpus luteum to start producing enough progesterone to make your temperature rise, and so what the time lag is between ovulation and the rise in your temperature. This makes it quite unproductive to try to time intercourse to coincide with ovulation, to try to beat the clock each month. Sperm can survive in the woman's reproductive organs for some time, and so if you really want to devise a timetable for intercourse, a better strategy is to have intercourse every other day around the time of ovulation.

OTHER TESTS OF OVULATION

The BBT gives an impression of whether you are ovulating, but it is not a precise measure.[3] So even though your temperature chart may indicate that you are ovulating, you may be given a more sensitive test of ovulation such as a blood progesterone test or an endometrial biopsy. The blood progesterone test is an easy and painless test, done in the second part of your cycle. A small amount of blood is taken and analysed to measure the amount of progesterone present. If the progesterone level is very low, then it is unlikely that you have ovulated. There are a number of reasons why your blood progesterone level may be low. The pituitary or hypothalamus in your brain may not be producing the hormones necessary to stimulate your ovaries to work and so you fail to ovulate. On the other hand, the brain may be producing the hormones but the ovaries themselves may not be responding to the hormones in the blood. Analysing the levels of hormones in your blood allows the laboratory to decide where exactly the problem may lie in your case.

Another possibility is that although you are producing sufficient quantities of progesterone, the second part of your cycle, the luteal phase, is too short. In this case the endometrium does not have time to build up, nor the fertilised egg time to implant and begin to grow before the cycle ends. This is called an inadequate luteal phase. Another indication of this might be short menstrual cycles.

Endometrial biopsy
Here a small sample of the endometrium is taken and examined. The procedure used is very similar to that employed in a D and C (dilation and curettage). A thin metal tube is inserted through the cervix into your uterus. The tube, or curettage, is then withdrawn, taking with it a small amount of the uterine lining. It can be an uncomfortable procedure, and is one which many doctors perform only under a general anaesthetic. So it requires you to become a hospital patient, if only for a short time. For this reason it is a test which is usually performed when you are already undergoing another test, such as a laparoscopy for which you are hospitalised and given a general anaesthetic.

Endometrial tissues formed after ovulation and under the influence of progesterone look different from those produced under the influence of oestrogen early in the cycle. So, by examining the endometrium it is possible to say whether hormones have been produced in sufficient quantities and therefore to deduce whether you have ovulated. The endometrium builds up under the influence of progesterone in a very consistent and predictable manner, so the state of the uterus and its readiness to accept a fertilised egg can be assessed at the same time.

TREATMENT: INDUCTION OF OVULATION

In from one-fifth to a quarter of infertility cases a hormonal problem resulting in failure to ovulate can be identified. There are a number of treatments now available for hormonal problems, and this is perhaps the area in which some of the most important advances in infertility treatment have been made. Which treatment is used and its chances of success depends upon the reasons why you do not ovulate. If you are not ovulating because of early ovarian failure, that is an early menopause, or because of damage done to your ovaries by radiotherapy or abdominal surgery, then there is little that can be done. However, if you are taking a long time to ovulate after coming off the pill, or you are not ovulating because of low levels of hormones then there is quite a good chance of boosting your hormone production and starting ovulation again. Two substances commonly used for this purpose are clomiphene citrate or clomiphene (marketed as Clomid) and human menopausal gonadotropin (HMG, marketed as Pergonal). About eight out of every ten women who are not ovulating successfully have their ovulation induced by the use of one of these drugs. The number of women who get pregnant is smaller, about five women out of every ten.

Clomid

Clomid was first discovered when drug companies were trying to produce new oestrogens for use in contraceptives. However, instead of suppressing ovulation, Clomid was found to induce it and it is now used very widely. It works by making the brain believe that the levels of oestrogen are very low and so it encourages the ovaries to produce more. It thus boosts the normal process whereby the brain stimulates the ovaries to produce oestrogen and the raised oestrogen level in turn stimulates the brain to produce the LH surge to trigger ovulation.

Clomid is taken as tablets in the first part of the cycle, for five days, usually from days 5 to 9. Ovulation then follows about seven days later. So one effect of Clomid might be to lengthen your cycle if yours is usually quite a short one. If the Clomid does not induce ovulation then the dose may be increased or you may be given a booster injection of human chorionic gonadotropin (HCG, marketed at Pregnyl).

They put me on Clomid and temperature charts. I was on Clomid for about nine months. I certainly didn't ovulate every month or have a period. They increased the dose twice. And for the last two months I was having a booster shot of HCG, mid-cycle. They inject the HCG into my bottom, and that is very painful. A lot of that seemed to depend on the nurse who did it. Sometimes it was worse than others.

For women who do not have periods the Clomid is started on some arbitrarily chosen day.

I don't have a cycle, no periods. I just start taking the Clomid at any time. You take it for five days, picking any day as day 5. Then on day 22 you go back to the hospital for a blood test, and they test the progesterone level and tell you whether you ovulated. It takes a fortnight to get the results. When I'm theoretically ten days overdue I trot along for a pregnancy test. If I'm not pregnant I start taking the Clomid again. I've been on the Clomid for five months now but I haven't ovulated yet.

Clomid is also given quite frequently to women who show signs of ovulation to try to boost the levels of hormones so that the endometrium might be better prepared to accept a fertilised egg, or to extend the second part of a cycle. 'He said I'm not quite sure whether you are ovulating or not so you might as well take the Clomid. I took it for six months.'

Clomid is being used here in an empirical way. To know whether it is having the desired effect, you need to have your progesterone level tested in the second part of your cycle to see whether it is any higher than in the cycles prior to taking the Clomid. Unfortunately such tests are rarely done.

The effect of Clomid lasts only for the cycle in which it is given; it does not have any long-term effects on ovulation nor on hormone levels. Clomid has a number of side-effects, and so some doctors are loathe to prescribe it for longer than three months. Others prescribe it for longer, up to nine months. These side effects include hot flushes and feelings of nausea or giddiness and some drying up of the cervical mucus. The quality of your cervical mucus is very important so you may be given oestrogen tablets to take together with Clomid to counteract its effect on your mucus. There is also a slightly greater chance of having twins when taking Clomid because the extra stimulation of your ovaries may make two eggs develop.

When you take Clomid, you also take other steps to maximise your chances of conceiving. This entails monitoring your body, probably using the BBT, to pinpoint the best time to have intercourse. Going to so much effort can make you anxious and tense.

When I was on Clomid I did get very upset because he was getting so fed up being ordered to perform to order. We were only given tablets for three months. The first time we had sex at the right time. The second time he had to go to work all night, which drove me mad. The next time he got absolutely blind drunk. He arranged it so he wasn't available. I had gone through all this and made all these efforts and he was trying to sabotage my attempts. I accused him of not wanting a baby at all but he said it wasn't that. He said it was having an effect on him too and that he would rather not be around than not be able to make it.

You may have great hopes that Clomid will solve your infertility problems and so feel very disappointed when it does not work and you fail to conceive.

After the first month on Clomid I thought I was pregnant. I was high thinking I was pregnant, but I wasn't. I was disappointed. I was so obsessed with it, I was almost hysterical. I thought I've got to slow down. I'm not watching the symptoms so much now. In the first month I was watching every sensation, every symptom, everything changing.

Pergonal
If Clomid does not induce ovulation then you may be given Pergonal. Pergonal consists of FSH and LH obtained from the urine of menopausal women who produce and secrete large amounts of these hormones. Pergonal works directly on the ovaries, inducing ovulation in perhaps two women out of three. Because Pergonal works in this way, it is more

difficult to control ovulation and sometimes two, three and even more eggs may develop and be released from the ovary.

Pergonal is more complicated to administer than Clomid; it involves going back to the hospital frequently and having your hormone levels monitored continuously. Pergonal cannot be taken orally but has to be injected. Frequently it is given for seven to ten days, and its effects on your oestrogen production are carefully monitored by testing your urine. This entails collecting all your urine over a 24-hour period for the duration of the injections and taking it every day to the hospital for analysis. When your oestrogen levels have increased sufficiently you are given a booster to trigger ovulation. The stimulant used is the hormone human chorionic gonadotropin (HCG) which acts in the same way as LH in a normal cycle. You are advised to have intercourse on that day and on subsequent days.

In *Why Children?* Anna Wileman talks about her experiences of Pergonal treatment.[4]

At first my hormone count was almost totally unresponsive to the Pergonal. After a week I became thoroughly tired of the whole thing. I asked if I could back out and go home... He allowed me to go home and have a district nurse complete the course, provided I continued to wee into bottles and bring the dirty great steaming containers into the hospital with me everyday. This I did. There followed a hilarious period when I had to smuggle jugs, funnels and plastic bottles into the school where I was teaching, conceal them under a pile of rubbish in the ladies and sneak out during lessons to perform the strange ritual of collecting every drop I passed.

The Pergonal worked, and Anna ovulated and conceived.

There are two important side effects of Pergonal. One is the slight risk of damage to the ovaries through over-stimulation; the other is multiple pregnancy. In up to a quarter of pregnancies following Pergonal treatment, there is more than one foetus, usually twins, occasionally triplets and on very rare occasions even more. You may not feel that the risk of having twins is a deterrent to using Pergonal, but multiple pregnancies are associated with greater risks such as miscarriage and premature births. (These are discussed in chapters 8 and 9.)

I'd got so excited about the Pergonal because one of the side effects is to have multiple births. I thought that was fantastic, a whole family at once. It was the first real hope we'd had.

Prolactin

Recently, it was discovered that failure to ovulate is sometimes caused by an excessively high level of prolactin, a hormone produced by the pituitary gland. Prolactin triggers the production of milk in the breasts and so a woman who is breast feeding produces greatly increased levels of prolactin.

A high level of prolactin in the blood can suppress ovulation. Other symptoms may be no periods and a milky discharge from the breasts. But you can have a high prolactin level and not display these symptoms. It is not clear why some women have such a level; sometimes it is associated with benign (non-malignant) pituitary tumour, or more rarely with thyroid or kidney problems. Your prolactin level may also be raised if you are taking certain tranquillisers.

A high prolactin level can be detected by a blood test. If you are not ovulating you may be tested early in your investigations or later, when Clomid fails to work. If you appear to be ovulating, your prolactin level may not be checked until after you have been through a whole range of tests and treatments.

> After months of post-coital tests, and all the other tests as well, they decided to do a blood test. And that's when I discovered that I had a high prolactin count. When they found that they were so pleased that they had found something wrong. She sent me off that minute down to the X-ray department so my pituitary could be X-rayed. Then she gave me the bromocriptine. I keep thinking of how things could have been different if they had thought of it sooner.

Once a high prolactin level has been diagnosed, the first step prior to any treatment is to check whether or not you have a pituitary tumour. This can be done by taking an X-ray of your skull and by checking your sight, as a tumour may sometimes press on your optic nerves and affect your sight. In rare cases, the tumour is removed surgically, but more often it is treated by the same drug given to suppress the production of prolactin, bromocriptine (marketed as Parlodel). This reduces the prolactin level to normal within a cycle or two. Once the prolactin levels are normal, most women ovulate, or ovulate more effectively. The success rate of bromocriptine is high; nine out of ten women who take it ovulate and seven out of ten become pregnant. As soon as you get a positive pregnancy test you are usually told to stop taking the bromocriptine. This means that in early pregnancy the prolactin level is higher than it is in most other pregnant women, but there does not seem to be a higher risk of miscarriage.

Bromocriptine is taken in tablet form and so it is easy to administer. The only side-effect appears to be that you may feel sick.

Like the other ovulation inducing hormones, bromocryptine is effective only in the cycles in which it is taken; it does not alter permanently your prolactin levels.

ORGANS OF REPRODUCTION

To conceive and maintain a pregnancy your reproductive organs must work effectively, so that the egg, the sperm and then the fertilised egg can travel along the Fallopian tubes and implant in the uterus. Figure 6.4 shows the organs that make up the reproductive system in women, and Figure 6.5 shows what is needed for conception to take place.

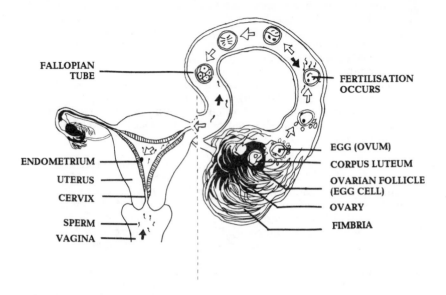

Figure 6.4 Women's reproductive organs

The ovaries: The ovaries are about the shape and size of an unshelled almond, and are held in place in the pelvic cavity by connecting tissues. The ovaries produce eggs, as well as the hormones oestrogen and progesterone which we discussed earlier in this chapter.

The Fallopian tubes: The Fallopian tubes are muscular tubes connecting the ovaries with the uterus. The ends of the Fallopian tubes are funnel-shaped with fingers called 'fimbria' which move around and pick up the egg as it is released from the ovaries; the egg travels along the Fallopian tube helped by contractions of the muscles, where it meets the sperm, and is fertilised. The fertilised egg makes its way to the uterus.

The uterus: The uterus is pear-shaped, with the Fallopian tubes entering it at the wide part, the horn, at the top, and with the cervix projecting into the vagina. The uterus is made of muscle which can expand to make space for a growing foetus. It is lined with endometrial tissue which grows under the influence of the female sex hormones either to be shed each cycle at menstruation or to provide sustenance for the foetus during pregnancy.

The cervix: The end of the uterus, where it protrudes into the vagina, is called the cervix. Like the uterus the cervix is made of muscle which normally stays tightly closed. But during labour it opens up to allow the baby to be born. The cervix also has an important part to play in conception. It produces mucus which is usually sticky to prevent bacteria entering the uterus. However, around the time of ovulation, as the levels of oestrogen increase, the cervical mucus becomes more watery, making it easier for the sperm to enter the uterus and meet the egg in the Fallopian tube. (We discuss the role of the cervical mucus in conception in chapter 7.)

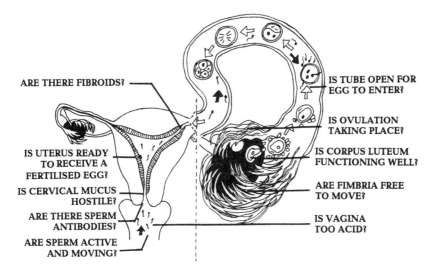

ARE THERE FIBROIDS?

IS TUBE OPEN FOR EGG TO ENTER?

IS OVULATION TAKING PLACE?

IS UTERUS READY TO RECEIVE A FERTILISED EGG?

IS CORPUS LUTEUM FUNCTIONING WELL?

IS CERVICAL MUCUS HOSTILE?

ARE FIMBRIA FREE TO MOVE?

ARE THERE SPERM ANTIBODIES?

IS VAGINA TOO ACID?

ARE SPERM ACTIVE AND MOVING?

Figure 6.5 What is needed for conception to take place

INVESTIGATION OF THE REPRODUCTIVE ORGANS

There are a number of tests of your reproductive organs. Each one involves a different procedure and gives different information. Some, such as the laparoscopy, are more informative but more costly and more complex to administer so they tend to be used only after the less sensitive tests have been tried. Others give less precise information. They may tell you that you have a condition which affects one or all of your reproductive organs, and which makes you infertile, such as endometriosis. Or they may tell you that you have an abnormality which is not clearly a bar to conception, such as fibroids. We describe the different tests below.

Physical examination: At your first appointment you are usually given a physical examination, including an internal examination. From this it is possible to gain some fairly straightforward information, for instance of congenital abnormalities, that is, an abnormality you were born with. One such abnormality is an absence of a uterus. Other problems may occasionally be detected, such as fibroids, a retroverted (backward-tilting) uterus, endometriosis, enlarged ovaries or an infection of your cervix. Usually other tests are needed to confirm that you have any one of these problems.

Tubal insufflation test (also called Rubin's test): Carbon dioxide is blown through your uterus and Fallopian tubes and the gas pressure is measured. If the tubes are clear the gas passes through the tubes into the pelvic cavity, and the gas pressure drops. The gas in the pelvic cavity may feel like a pain in your shoulder. If the tubes are blocked the gas stays in your uterus and the pressure stays high. Although this test can tell you whether there is a blockage it gives no information about where it might be, so if you seem to have a blockage you will probably be given another test, such as an HSG or a laparoscopy to locate it. Because the information gained from the test is so imprecise it appears to be used much less frequently than it once was. Some doctors still like to use it because they believe that the pressure of the gas in the tubes may shift any minor adhesions or blockages. It may be given at the same time as other tests which require a general anaesthetic, such as an endometrial biopsy.

Hysterosalpingram: The hysterosalpingram, often referred to as HSG, is an X-ray of the uterus and Fallopian tubes. Its name is derived from the words for uterus (hystero), Fallopian tubes (salpingo) and picture (gram). A radio-opaque dye is introduced through the cervix and its progress through the uterus into the Fallopian tubes and out into the pelvic cavity is observed using X-rays. X-rays are absorbed by the soft tissues of the reproductive system and so a dye must be used which reflects them back, thereby giving a picture of the system. The HSG is a useful test; it gives a lot of information about the state of the uterus and the Fallopian tubes. Consequently, it is used quite commonly.

The test is done on about Day 10 of your cycle, after your period ends and before you ovulate. It is not done during your period because pushing the endometrium into the Fallopian tubes and into the pelvic cavity could cause infection or even endometriosis. It is done before you ovulate so that there is no chance of the dye, with its small amount of radioactive material, interfering with a fertilised egg. You are asked to ring to make an appointment on the first day of your period so that the test can be timed properly. If your period is very long or your cycle is short it is clearly important to tell the hospital when you book in for the HSG.

An HSG is usually performed on an out-patient basis in the X-ray department. At some hospitals it is done under a general anaesthetic. As we believe that 'forewarned is forearmed', we must tell you that the HSG can be painful. In fact, it is probably the most painful of the procedures used in infertility investigations. Many of the books on infertility and the doctors themselves underestimate the discomfort experienced by women undergoing the HSG.[5] This approach can make it more unpleasant.

If anything hurts that they haven't told me about, I automatically think that something has gone wrong, that something's happened that shouldn't have happened. I think that just to reassure you, they should tell you. Quite a high proportion of pain is when you are tense, and obviously you are going to be tense when something is hurting, but you can do something about it if that's how you know it's going to be. I thought something terrible had happened.

Some doctors believe that if you forewarn women about the pain they may experience from the HSG they may not turn up for the appointment. But it is an important test and for most women undergoing infertility investigations, the benefits of the test outweigh the discomfort and so we feel sure that they will attend, but they will be better prepared. In fact, if the doctors themselves would acknowledge the discomfort they were causing during the HSG, it might enable women to bear the pain more easily.

Our advice to women going for an HSG is to get someone to come with you to the hospital; do not drive there yourself. Leave the rest of the day free. If you do find the test painful, then you are in the best position to deal with it, and if you do not, then you can have a day out together. Take some painkillers with you in case you are not offered any. Some women lose some of the dye afterwards or bleed, so you might want to take a sanitary towel with you.

When you arrive at the X-ray department, you are asked to strip off and put on a hospital gown. Inside the X-ray room, you lie on your back on a table. Above the table is the X-ray machinery, alongside is a TV monitor sceen which the radiographer watches. You may be allowed to watch the monitor too – ask them if they do not offer. It really is exciting to see the outline of your uterus and your tubes. 'The only thing that I thought was good about it was seeing the television. I found that good. I thought, that's my womb. That was exciting.'

You are prepared for the X-ray. This is done by creating a sterile field to minimise the chances of introducing an infection. A speculum is inserted into your vagina. Then a cannula, or a thin tube, is passed through your cervix into the uterus. Through this the dye is pumped. The progress of the dye is watched on the television monitor and permanent records are made. The whole procedure may take about 20 to 30 minutes. Occasionally, your muscles go into spasm, contracting suddenly and blocking the progress of the dye. If this happens you may be given a muscle relaxant.

What information do we get from an HSG?: The HSG can point to problems of the uterus or of the Fallopian tubes. The most common problem of the uterus is fibroids (discussed later in this chapter). Very occasionally structural abnormalities of the uterus may be found, such as a double uterus separated completely or incompletely by a septum. Such abnormalities of the uterus may affect your ability to carry through a pregnancy rather than your ability to conceive (this is discussed in chapter 8). Structural abnormalities are sometimes corrected surgically.

The HSG is probably most important because it shows the condition (or patency) of your Fallopian tubes. If your tubes are patent the dye passes through them and spills out into the pelvic cavity and you can see it form clouds on the television monitor.

If one or both of your tubes are blocked, the dye is not able to pass into the pelvic cavity; instead it stops at the point of obstruction. Tubal problems can sometimes be treated with surgery.

Sometimes it is thought that the HSG itself can serve as a treatment. There is evidence of a slightly higher chance of conceiving in the two or three cycles following an HSG.[6] This probably happens because the pressure of the dye passing through the tubes clears some small adhesions and so improves their patency.

About half of the women who undergo the HSG are found to have nothing wrong and the search for the cause of their infertility moves on to other things. Should your HSG indicate that there is some problem, you may be investigated further before any treatment is suggested. A laparoscopy may be performed to enable the gynaecologist to take a closer look and to check that the problem discovered by the HSG is not in fact a complication or technical hiccup caused by the procedure itself – a not uncommon occurrence.

Laparoscopy: In this test your reproductive organs are observed directly. A laparoscopy is usually performed in the second part of the cycle, so that ovulation can also be confirmed. It is carried out under a general anaesthetic so usually you are hospitalised for two or three days. Very occasionally, a laparoscopy is given under a local anaesthetic.

A small incision is made, just below your umbilicus or belly button. Carbon dioxide gas is then pumped into your stomach, to push out the abdominal wall and separate the organs so they can be observed more clearly. A thin telescope, equipped with its own light source, is then inserted through the same incision. This allows the ovaries, the outside of the uterus and the Fallopian tubes to be examined. Often a dye is also pumped into the uterus, as in the HSG, to check whether the dye passes through the tubes and into the pelvic cavity.

The surgery involved is minor, although there are always slight risks in having a general anaesthetic. The only discomfort caused is by the gas, which is gradually absorbed, but which can collect for a time at the top of your pelvic cavity and be experienced as shoulder pain. 'For two or three days I felt I had been kicked in the shoulder, but apart from that it wasn't bad.'

The small incision made near your umbilicus is repaired with a stitch or two. These are usually removed before you leave the hospital, leaving a small mark no more than a centimetre in length.

You are generally given the results of your operation soon afterwards, while you are still in hospital.

All the minor operations were done by the surgeon on a Friday.

You went in on the Thursday, had the operation on the Friday, and then you had your chat with the doctor the next morning. And he had the unenviable task of going round the ward and telling each woman where she stood. It isn't an easy situation, you feel so tense. He was very good about saying what he had found, he came straight to the point.

It is good to have this rapid feedback and it contrasts pleasantly with the long delays frequently experienced in getting the results of other tests.

You are probably on a ward with other women having gynaecological operations, sometimes with women having abortions. This can be a painful experience both for the infertile women and for those having an abortion.

I found the laparoscopy a pretty horrifying time. The ward was full of women having hysterectomies, abortions or women having problems with their pregnancies. I was admitted together with two women having abortions and two being sterilised. I had an idea that the ones being sterilised would have the same cut as me. On the way down to the theatre I said, please don't do the wrong operation on me. One of the girls having an abortion was about sixteen, she said she felt terrible that I couldn't have children and that she was having an abortion. I told her there is no point in feeling guilty and that I would probably have the abortion in her position. But I did find it difficult.

You may find the experience less difficult to handle.

When I had my operation there were women there having abortions and things like that. It's not something that troubled me too much. I suppose I thought the operation would work.

We think that more care should be taken to keep women having infertility investigations and women having abortions in separate wards whenever that is possible, for both their sakes.

On the whole, however, the laparoscopy is a procedure about which you may feel quite positive. Being in hospital may bring you into contact with other women having infertility investigations, and you may find this a supportive experience.

We could all hear everyone else's affairs and we were all listening like anything. We all chattered together and sat on one another's beds. We swopped experiences. The motive for us being there was that we all wanted to conceive. It was a terrific bond. Each woman propped up the other at times when they needed it.

Going into hospital gives your problem some recognition; you, and those around you, can feel now that there is something wrong. You can be treated as a proper patient, being visited, brought flowers, and needing time to recover. We all appreciate having a fuss made of us sometimes and that may more than compensate for any discomforts of the laparoscopy.

What do we learn from a laparoscopy?: By looking directly at your reproductive organs a firm answer can be given to a number of questions. Often, no problem is identified and your investigation moves on to other things. A number of problems may be found. Adhesions and scars obstructing the passage of the egg from the ovary to the Fallopian tube can be observed. The laparoscopy gives a picture of the outside of the tubes and of the fimbria and provides more information on which to base decisions about operating. Fibroids positioned on the outside of the uterus can be inspected and assessed. Endometriosis and polycystic ovaries can be diagnosed conclusively only in this way.

PROBLEMS OF THE REPRODUCTIVE ORGANS AND THEIR TREATMENTS

Fibroids: Fibroids, known technically as myoma, are benign (non-cancerous) tumours found in nearly one in five women of reproductive age.[7] They may be situated outside, inside, or within the uterine wall. The sort of problems they present depends on how large they are and where they are situated. Symptoms such as heavy and painful periods may indicate fibroids. However, many women with fibroids have successful pregnancies and their presence is not always considered a problem.

Fibroids can usually be detected by an internal examination, but some may be more difficult to discover. An HSG gives a clear picture of the fibroids inside your uterus, where they are and how large they are, and a laparoscopy gives information about any fibroids on the outside of your uterus. Fibroids can be a fertility problem if they are situated near the entrance to the uterus from the Fallopian tubes. Here they may block the passage of the egg from the tube into the uterus. Fibroids may also cause problems in pregnancy, as they grow bigger during that time. If they are bulky they may obstruct the growth of the foetus or restrict its blood supply and so cause miscarriage. Where fibroids are considered a fertility problem, they are removed surgically. This operation, an abdominal myomectomy, is quite a serious one and is not popular amongst surgeons. You may have to shop around before you find a gynaecologist willing to perform it. After this operation, most gynaecologists recommend that babies are delivered by Caesarean section, because of the scarring and subsequent weakness of the muscle wall.

Polycystic ovaries: This is a fairly unusual condition in which the ovaries develop many small cysts and may become enlarged.[8] Why this should happen is not entirely clear, but it is probably caused by an imbalance in the production of the hormones LH and FSH. The result is that the egg cells in the ovary do not develop properly and cannot break away from the ovary but instead form cysts. This lack of ovulation is sometimes, but certainly not always, associated with other symptoms, the most common of which are having more body hair (hirsutism), obesity and having no periods. Because women with polycystic ovaries often have no periods, they may seek medical help for this problem and only think about having children later.

I rarely had periods, just once in a blue moon. I went to the doctor when I was seventeen and was told that I was probably just a late developer. Well, eventually I went back again. They did blood tests and then I had a laparoscopy and they told me that I had cysts on both ovaries and that one was slightly enlarged.

Other women go for infertility advice and discover that they have polycystic ovaries.

If the ovaries are enlarged, they may be detected in a physical examination. A blood test detects unusual levels of hormones, but polycystic ovaries can be diagnosed conclusively only after a laparoscopy.

Two kinds of treatment can be offered; one hormonal and one surgical. The hormonal treatment involves ovulation-inducing hormones, generally starting with Clomid and then moving on to Pergonal and HCG if the Clomid does not work. These hormones do seem to work with a large proportion of women; eight out of ten women ovulate, and four of the ten get pregnant. If hormone therapy fails to induce ovulation, surgical treatment may be considered. This consists of removing a small wedge-shaped section of the ovary. After this the ovary is often more responsive to hormones and so the eggs can develop and leave the ovaries successfully. With abdominal surgery there is always a risk of scars and adhesions developing which may reduce the chances of pregnancy, and so it is better to start with hormonal treatments.

Both these treatments have only short-term effects. The ovulation-inducing hormones work only in the cycles in which they are given; they do not get the ovaries working again normally. The wedge resection operation has longer lasting effects; it is possible to ovulate and to get pregnant up to a year after the operation. Because the treatments have only relatively short-lived effects and do not restore the general functioning of your ovaries, they are of benefit only to women who want to get pregnant and do not offer help to women who seek relief from any other symptoms. You may be advised to get pregnant quickly because the longer the problem continues the less successful is the treatment.

This puts pressure on you to make a rapid decision about your fertility.

We had both assumed that because I didn't have periods I was infertile. So when I had the tests, they said there are various things you can do and we recommend that you do them straight away – because the condition gets worse, or at least it becomes less rectifiable with time. So they recommended that I start immediately. At that point I wasn't too interested in doing it, mainly because I still felt there was plenty of time. So I went away and thought about it and decided to try.

Endometriosis: Endometriosis is a strange disease. Doctors have little idea of its cause or of the number of women who suffer from it although some suggest that the number could be as high as one in ten.[9] What happens is that endometrium, the tissue which is normally found in the uterus, appears in patches elsewhere, usually in the pelvic cavity, on the ovaries, the pelvic wall, the appendix, or even in the bowel and bladder. Here, this misplaced (medically called ectopic) endometrium undergoes the same cyclical changes as the endometrium in the uterus – that is, it builds up during the menstrual cycle and is shed during menstruation. The problem is that the menstrual blood from the misplaced endometrium has nowhere to escape to and so it is shed into the pelvic cavity where it irritates the normal tissue or forms cysts and scar tissue which may cause adhesions.

One of the strange things about endometriosis is that the severity of your symptoms has little to do with how extensively you have it. Some women may have severe pain but few patches, others have many patches but only mild symptoms. Where it is located determines to a large extent the kind of symptoms you may experience, for example, if your bowel is affected, you will probably have bouts of constipation, diahorrhea and rectal bleeding around the time of your period, but then again, you may not. The typical symptoms are painful periods, irregular periods and painful intercourse. The symptoms are less severe or disappear immediately following your period and they increase and are most severe during menstruation.

Endometriosis and infertility: Infertility is included as a symptom of endometriosis. However, women with endometriosis arrive at infertility clinics in one of two ways: there are those who experience difficulty in conceiving and during the course of their infertility investigations are discovered to be suffering from endometriosis. These women may be very surprised to learn that they have it, partly because they have few symptoms and partly because very few women know of the disease beforehand.

> The difficulty about endometriosis is that I never had irregular periods. I have always been remarkably regular. I've never had much pain or tenderness. So I wasn't alerted to the fact that anything was wrong in a very dramatic way. That is the most difficult way of going to get help. You never know whether you're imagining it or not.

The other group of women are those who have endometriosis and are advised that the best cure is to conceive and are attending infertility clinics to help them to do so. These women may not wish to have a child, or their personal circumstances may be such that pregnancy would normally be out of the question and yet they are told that pregnancy is the most effective treatment for their disease. Infertility investigations for these women can be a profoundly confusing experience.

One consultant said, if you want children you've got to get

pregnant within the next year, but your chances are very low. I don't want to have a child for that reason. I can't justify bringing a child into the world to cure my endometriosis.

Why it causes infertility is unclear. For women with severe endometriosis, their Fallopian tubes may be so damaged that it is impossible for the egg to reach the sperm. Other women may have 'chocolate' cysts on their ovaries which impair ovulation. But even where it is mild or where the endometrium is not found on the tubes or ovaries, women can remain infertile. Several theories have been proposed to explain this. One is the 'Delilah' theory which suggests that the misplaced endometrium seduces the egg shed at ovulation and therefore it does not travel down the Fallopian tube to meet the sperm but gets lost within the pelvic cavity. Another, perhaps more scientific view, is that women with endometriosis do not ovulate properly because of hormonal problems; this is the most widely held theory and has implications for treatment.

How endometriosis is diagnosed and treated: It can be difficult to get endometriosis diagnosed. Some women have to persevere to get their doctors to accept that there is anything wrong with them – that they are not just complaining about normal menstrual symptoms. There are two things you can do to maximise your chances of diagnosis. The first is to chart your symptoms to see when they occur. Sometimes your doctor may ask you to do this. If you have tangible proof that you have not imagined your symptoms, you may be less likely to be sent away as 'neurotic' and you are better able to deal with this kind of reaction. The second thing is to try to see your doctor during the second half of your cycle when your symptoms are most obvious. Endometriosis can sometimes be felt by an internal examination but it can be overlooked if this examination is too soon after the end of your period when the endometriosis is least noticeable. The most conclusive test is to observe it by laparoscopy. This enables the gynaecologist to visualise the condition of your ovaries and Fallopian tubes and to assess the severity of your endometriosis. Unfortunately, some women have such severe symptoms that they may be admitted to hospital for emergency treatment.

The treatment you are offered depends on how old you are, whether you have children, how extensive the disease is, and the approach of your doctor.

There are two approaches to treatment: medical and surgical. Medical treatment is based on the fact that misplaced endometrium follows the same changes as endometrium in the uterus. During pregnancy or menopause the endometrium does not build up or get shed. So the idea is to induce these states by administering drugs, or for the woman to become pregnant. Menstruation will then stop for a number of months, allowing the patches of misplaced endometrium to dry up, and hopefully to disappear altogether. Nowadays the drug therapy most often prescribed is Danazol. This induces menopausal symptoms. It can have side effects, such as hot flushes, weight gain, acne and hirsutism (hairiness), but doctors assure us that most women are prepared to put up with them. It is a treatment which works well for some women. After a number of months on drug therapy, women are taken off the treatment. If they want children, they can try to conceive. As we mentioned earlier, it is thought that women with endometriosis have problems in ovulating and they are sometimes prescribed drugs to stimulate ovulation. These drugs work by increasing hormone levels and also stimulate the endometrium, both in the uterus and the misplaced endometrium, sometimes causing a recurrence of symptoms.

Surgical treatment is either conservative or radical. Conservative treatment aims to remove as much of the misplaced endometrium as possible and to restore the pelvic organs to health again, thereby enabling the woman to conceive. This treatment is usually favoured if patches of endometrium are found on the Fallopian tubes and ovaries. The results, in terms of pregnancies, seem quite optimistic but depend on other factors such as your age, how long and how badly you have had endometriosis. Your chances of conceiving are highest immediately following the operation.

Where pregnancy is not desired, medical treatment may be given after the operation. But the pressure to conceive after this may be considerable.

> I know it sounds weird, but I felt obliged to get pregnant. I felt that if I didn't pursue it, then they would no longer wish to treat the endometriosis conservatively. They might want to do something more drastic, like a hysterectomy which I really don't want.

Where the disease is extensive, radical surgery is advised. This is a hysterectomy where the ovaries are removed as well and you may be given hormone replacement therapy. The uterus itself is not affected by the disease and some women may find it strange to have a healthy organ removed to cure a disease elsewhere. It is the one kind of treatment which is guaranteed to cure endometriosis, but naturally it is one which women try to avoid. But when the disease is so severe, and your chance of conceiving very slim, the relief from pain and ill health may give you new energy and a new lease of life. 'I used to look terrible, at least ten years older than I was. To be honest, it's only since I've had the hysterectomy that I've discovered that sex is rather nice. I used to loathe it, it was so painful.'

Damaged Fallopian tubes: The Fallopian tubes can be damaged in different ways, and the severity of that damage can vary from woman to woman.

The Fallopian tubes are particularly prone to infections such as PID (pelvic inflammatory disease) or salpingitis. Sometimes infections start up after having VD, after childbirth, an abortion or after having pelvic surgery, and they are more common in women who are using an IUD. Once the infection has cleared up, scar tissue or adhesions may remain which can block the ends or the body of the tube or can damage the muscle fibres so that the tube is no longer able to work efficiently. Adhesions or bands of connective tissue can also form round the outside of the tube after an infection. These may immobilise the tube, making it difficult for it to transport the egg. One or both tubes may be damaged; if both are damaged the egg cannot reach the uterus. If only one is damaged a pregnancy is still possible, although it might take longer. The same conditions can damage the fimbria so that the delicate folds or fingers stick together and are unable to move around freely. In severe cases, they may be drawn together completely, blocking off the end of the tube. Pelvic infections do not always lead to blocked tubes, but it makes sense to report them so that you can be tested early in your investigations. Identifying a problem in your reproductive system does not mean that you will necessarily be any wiser about how the problem developed. You may search through your life to try and find the cause, and seize on one event which offers a valid explanation, perhaps an abortion – even though there is often no evidence that that is to blame.[10]

Treatment of damaged Fallopian tubes: Sometimes it is possible to remove scar tissue and adhesions using surgery. The procedure is similar to that employed in a laparoscopy. An incision is made near the umbilicus through which carbon dioxide gas is pumped and then the laparoscope is inserted. Another small incision is made lower down the abdomen through which the surgical instruments are introduced to repair the damage. This involves removal of tissue from around the ovaries, the fimbria or from the outside of the Fallopian tubes. On other occasions it is necessary to do more substantial surgery, such as removal of the blocked parts of the Fallopian tubes or opening up the ends of the tubes and tying them back to make a passage for the egg.

The development of the techniques of microsurgery which allow such delicate operations to take place constitutes a significant breakthrough in the treatment of infertility. The rate of success can be anything from 15 per cent to 65 per cent depending on how extensive is the scarring and which parts of the system are affected. It is easier to restore the main body of the tube to working order than it is to restore the more delicate fimbria. If the damage to the fimbria is very substantial then the chances of conception after surgery are low.

The fimbria and the tubes function not only by giving the egg a clear passage to the uterus, but also by helping it along its way. The fimbria move around and catch the egg and the tube moves it along by a series of contractions. Surgery can now often clear a passage for the egg, but there is no guarantee that the tubes will be able to contract efficiently afterwards. And with any kind of surgery there is always the risk of creating new scars and adhesions.

The success rate also depends on whether conception or live births is taken as the measure of success. The incidence of tubal or ectopic pregnancy is greater after tubal surgery. An ectopic pregnancy is one which begins to develop in the Fallopian tube rather than in the uterus. An ectopic pregnancy cannot continue within the Fallopian tube as the tube cannot stretch to accommodate it, and bursts eventually. An ectopic pregnancy, therefore, has to be removed surgically as soon as possible, and hopefully before it damages the tube too severely.

An ectopic pregnancy can be difficult to diagnose. You have the same early signs of pregnancy; missed period, tender breasts and slightly softened and enlarged uterus. So an internal examination may not necessarily detect it. However, as the egg grows, the tube stretches slightly and you feel cramps or a constant dull abdominal pain. If the tube bursts you bleed inside, and the pain continues. If you experience any of these symptoms you should seek help quickly.

In vitro fertilisation (IVF): This is the procedure known as creating test-tube babies although test tubes are not used.[11] So far, it has been offered to women whose only fertility problem is blocked Fallopian tubes but some gynaecologists forecast that it will be offered to women with other fertility problems. The egg is removed from the woman and combined with her partner's sperm in the laboratory. This is the 'test tube' part of the process. Once the egg has been fertilised, it is put into the woman's uterus to implant and grow. The process is complex and a whole range of techniques have been developed to make in vitro fertilisation possible. These include predicting and monitoring ovulation very carefully, finding the right mix of substances in which to keep the egg while it is fertilised and starting to develop, and discovering the best time and methods of putting the egg into the uterus to maximise the chances of its implanting. The development of these techniques increases our understanding of the processes of ovulation and implantation and so brings benefit to many other women. But because the process is so complicated the success rate to date is low. It is not clear how many women have become pregnant, but the number of live births from in vitro fertilisation is still very small. The procedure is being used more widely, both in Britain in several NHS hospitals, and in Germany, Austria and Australia where a number of live births have been reported.

It is the most complex and most disruptive of all the procedures we have described. It requires a stay in hospital during fertilisation, and extremely careful monitoring beforehand and afterwards to detect pregnancy. Part of this monitoring is necessary to test the new techniques which are changing all the time. Ovulation may be induced using Clomid or Perganol. Around the time the egg reaches the point of ovulation, hormone levels are carefully monitored, usually by measuring the hormones in your urine, to pinpoint the best time to remove the eggs from the ovaries. Under a general anaesthetic, the ovaries are inspected using a laparoscope and any ripe egg follicles are removed. These are then fertilised by sperm produced by the man in the hospital. If the eggs are fertilised they are allowed to grow for a time before being introduced into the uterus. For this, the cervix has to be dilated and obviously care has to be taken to prevent introducing an infection. Hopefully, the egg implants itself in the uterus. From this brief description it is clear that in vitro fertilisation involves a considerable amount of interference and monitoring for what is, as yet, a very low chance of success. But for many women, it does offer some hope of success and, given the opportunity, they are prepared to try it.

In vitro fertilisation would be a possibility for someone like me. They don't do it at the hospital I go to. I would be prepared to try it. I've gone through so much it would be worth it to have a baby of our own. I'd be prepared to pay for it.

One of the positive aspects of in vitro fertilisation is that it allows you to conceive and give birth to your partner's child. For women with blocked tubes where surgery has failed, the intrusiveness and the low success rate of in vitro fertilisation may not seem so daunting considering both the intrusiveness of adoption procedures and the very small number of babies available for adoption.

At present there is much concern expressed about the ethics of in vitro fertilisation. These concerns appear to centre around two areas. Firstly, there is concern about what happens to the eggs that are removed: in some cases a number of eggs are removed and may be fertilised. However, more eggs may get fertilised than it is thought advisable to return to the uterus, as multiple pregnancies are risky pregnancies. Some efforts have been made, as yet unsuccessfully, to freeze those eggs which are left. If this were done successfully, then if the first in vitro fertilisation failed or if the woman did not maintain her pregnancy, these fertilised eggs would be available and could give her a second chance at a pregnancy without having to go through all the business and the risks of inducing ovulation and removing the eggs for a second time. But what happens to these fertilised eggs if she does not need them or does not use them again? To allow them to die or to use them for research raises all kinds of moral issues. One possibility which has been discussed is to donate them to another woman, to introduce them into her uterus in the hope that she might in this way carry and give birth to a child, much like adoption but at an earlier stage. Parents then take on a fertilised egg which started life in another woman's body. It can seem like a very sisterly gesture for one woman who is being treated for infertility to be able to help another.

A second concern about in vitro fertilisation is the use of resources. The development of in vitro fertilisation is an expensive business, and one that at present is difficult to justify financially given the low rates of success. Some critics argue that scarce health resources should not be used in this way. While there is an unwillingness to maintain even current levels of investment in the health service, this is a powerful issue. Infertility is an important aspect of health care, one which affects the lives of a large number of women and men. IVF is not the only area around infertility which requires more investigation. We believe that a more vital priority is to look at the reasons why women are infertile, to suggest ways of reducing its incidence and to discover other forms of treatment. In particular in this area, we need to know more about the impact of the IUD on fertility, about ways of preventing tubal damage after surgery, after abortions and childbirth and of improving current techniques of tubal surgery. This kind of knowledge would have more to offer a greater number of women, and may reduce the numbers of women who look to in vitro fertilisation as the solution to their infertility. But there will never be one single good solution to women's infertility; we need medical research to develop in a number of parallel ways, so that eventually a range of solutions will be available.

There is great pressure on women to have children, and to concentrate their energies and their identities on their children: having children is seen as a large part of what is required for the health and happiness of women. This is why some women are willing to go to such elaborate efforts to have children, and why when they compare it with childlessness, some women see such treatment as an answer to their prayers. It is this pressure and these needs that we must understand and question as much as the medical solutions.

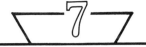

INFERTILITY IN MEN AND WOMEN:
COMPATIBILITY

In about one in three cases of infertility, the problem centres on the ability of sperm to survive in a woman's body, sometimes called a problem of compatability. For conception, sperm must be able to travel inside the woman's reproductive system to reach the egg and fertilise it. The survival of sperm within the woman's body depends on a number of factors: some relate to the sperm and some to the ability of the woman's body to tolerate them. In this chapter we look at these problems of compatability and at the treatments available.

WHAT IS NECESSARY FOR COMPATIBILITY

Certain interactions take place between the semen and the woman's body which are important if conception is to take place. After ejaculation, only a very few of the sperm deposited in the vagina, perhaps two hundred, actually reach the egg. The major loss is thought to arise through sperm leaving the vagina, a sort of leakage. This is a natural occurrence and not a cause of infertility. But the vagina itself is a naturally hostile environment for sperm and can become more hostile. Vaginal secretions are normally acid but this acidity is usually compensated for by the more alkaline seminal fluid. Seminal fluid provides some protection for sperm which can last up to two hours. Sperm have to move through the cervix into the uterus. Normally the cervix is plugged with mucus which protects the uterus from infection and which, at the same time, acts as a barrier to sperm. This cervical mucus is a thick, opaque substance. At ovulation, the mucus becomes thinner, clearer and more àbundant and allows sperm to pass through. It stretches out like an elastic band between your fingers. These changes in consistency are controlled by the production of oestrogen which reaches its peak prior to ovulation. After ovulation progesterone makes the mucus return to its tacky state. Sperm motility is also important if the sperm are to leave the hostile environment of the vagina and to pass through the cervical mucus into the uterus. After this the woman's own body helps it along to the Fallopian tubes. The woman's body has an active role to play in conception, and is not merely a vessel waiting passively for the sperm to invade.

Sperm are thought to undergo a final stage of development in the woman's reproductive system called capacitation in which they acquire the capacity to fuse with the egg.

So for good compatibility, you need sufficient numbers of motile sperm which can survive in the woman's body, and for the woman's body to provide a welcoming environment.

THE INVESTIGATION OF COMPATIBILITY

The most frequently used test in infertility investigations is the post-coital test (PCT), sometimes known as the Sims-Huhner test. (Post-coital means after intercourse.) It is a test of the ability of the sperm to survive inside the woman, and, although a test of compatibility, just one of you, the woman, attends the clinic.

The PCT is carried out in the middle of your cycle, just prior to ovulation. Timing is of key importance here because the consistency of the cervical mucus changes very rapidly around ovulation according to the levels of oestrogen and progesterone. Wrong timing is a common reason for a poor post-coital test and so, before making an appointment for the test, you should consider carefully your cycle length and when you expect to ovulate, preferably using temperature charts. Unfortunately, in many clinics post-coital tests are done only once or twice a week which means that it may be extremely difficult to ensure that you are being tested at the time that is best for you.

Although the post-coital test has been used extensively for more than sixty years, there is still no uniformity in the way it is performed; so the instructions can vary from doctor to doctor. You are told to abstain from sexual intercourse for between two to four days and then to have intercourse some hours before the test. Clinics vary considerably in how long after intercourse they want to do the test and in how strictly they want you to keep to the times they specify. There is no right or wrong interval between intercourse and the test, although it is important to let them know how long it is since intercourse took place so they can bear that in mind when evaluating the mucus-sperm mix. So, if you really do not like having intercourse first thing in the morning, or you find it inconvenient, you should say so.

They told us to make love first thing in the morning and come in. Well, what if you don't feel like it? We're dreadful in the morning. We put the alarm on at six o'clock and we had the kettle there to make coffee. But we'd just lie there laughing, it was the last thing we felt like doing.

Having a post-coital test puts considerable pressure on you; pressure to make sure that you get the timing right, and then pressure to have intercourse for the test.

I really hated the post-coital test. It was horrid waking up at seven in the morning knowing you have to have sex. You've got to get the stuff into you and then get yourself to the hospital. He hated it and I hated making him do it.

You are the one who has to keep the appointment and so it is your responsibility to make sure the instructions are complied with.

I said, I've got an appointment at ten o'clock, we've just got to do it. He refused. We had a terrible argument. He kept saying that sex should be a thing of beauty. I just said, that's too bad, you've got to do it now. There's no time for a discussion. So eventually he stormed out. He left home. I remember him stomping to the end of the road, and as he went out, he knocked over the pot plant in the hall and the cat went scurrying and the soil went everywhere. That was at about three in the morning. Eventually he stormed back into the house and came to bed and we had another row. I kept saying he had to do it. Eventually he calmed down and agreed. I had to use a douche and while I was in the bathroom he made a cup of tea. Finally, we made it at about four in the morning.

Quite often, you may be unable to have intercourse. Then you have to phone up and cancel your appointment.

I had to make two appointments for the post-coital because the first time he couldn't do it. They were very nice about it and said it happens all the time. I'm glad we made it the second time because you get into more and more of a state. It just gets worse.

You may be asked to have a number of these tests, so the pressure on your sex life is extended over a period of months. So although the post-coital test is painless and physically unobtrusive, you may find it a very difficult test to go through because it can intrude badly on your relationship.

When you have intercourse for the test, you should consider using the techniques we describe in chapter 4. Some doctors see the post-coital test as an opportunity to assess your sexual technique. For instance, if they find no sperm, they might question whether you are doing it the right way.

It takes me about half an hour to get to the hospital. I lay in bed, I didn't even get up to have a pee in case I lost any sperm. I thought, I'll let them get right up there, well inside me before I get up. I lay there for about half an hour before I got up and rushed to the hospital, preserving every drop of his precious fluid. No one told me to do that, I just thought it made sense. When I got there, the doctor asked me if we'd done it right. I said, yes I think so.

At the clinic, a sample of your cervical mucus with sperm in it is removed for examination. This is done by inserting a tube, like a straw, through a speculum, and sucking out a small sample. (See figure 7.1.) The mucus is then placed on a slide and examined under a microscope. You may be allowed to have a look yourself, and it is well worth asking if you can do so.

She did show me the slide which was really nice. I saw several sperm swimming around like little tadpoles. I felt really pleased. But all the other times there was nothing to see and so she didn't bother to show me.

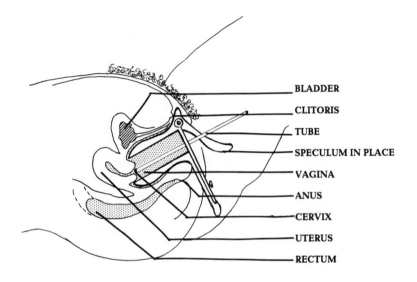

BLADDER

CLITORIS

TUBE

SPECULUM IN PLACE

VAGINA

ANUS

CERVIX

UTERUS

RECTUM

Figure 7.1 Post-coital test

If compatibility is not a problem, and the timing of the test is right, your mucus is clear and you should be able to see some sperm moving about quite freely. There is a lot of disagreement about the interpretation of the post-coital test. Some doctors argue that hours after intercourse, few healthy sperm should be found in the cervix; instead they should be in the uterus, on their way to the Fallopian tubes. Others argue that sperm do not have a built-in homing device aimed at the Fallopian tubes and may be found quite actively swimming near the cervix hours after intercourse, without signifying a problem.

The results of the post-coital test are available then and there.

When I went for the test, he scooped some stuff out and put it under the microscope. He said, 'This isn't very good.' I felt like saying, it's the best we could do. Instead I asked him what the problem was. He told me that there weren't many live sperm around. That was his only comment. We had to have another test.

Quite often, you are asked to do the test again on the next cycle or cycles, either to check the accuracy of the first, perhaps by improving on the timing of the test, or to assess the effectiveness of any treatment.

I had an endless process of post-coitals which became more and more degrading. I felt nothing much at all at first, but lately it's become very demeaning, just going in and opening my legs and going through all that again. The more it goes on, the more undermined I feel, and the less I want to go there each month.

If you have a poor post-coital test, some clinics carry out different tests to try and discover where the problem lies. If your partner has not yet had a semen test, he may be asked to have one at this point. The post-coital test is not a substitute for a semen test which gives somewhat different information. If he has had a semen test then there are still other tests which may be used. The simplest of these is the sperm-invasion test. For this, you are asked to provide both a sample of your own mucus at ovulation and a sample of your partner's sperm. Some of your mucus and some of his sperm is put together on a slide to examine the effects of your mucus on the motility of the sperm and the time it takes sperm to pass through the mucus.

A more complicated procedure is the cross-hostility test. Here the reaction of your mucus to different sperm and the motility of your partner's sperm in different mucus is examined. In this way, it may be possible to identify whether the incompatibility problems lies with you or with your partner. But this procedure can be carried out only in a clinic where a number of post-coital tests take place regularly and where there is a supply of sperm and mucus samples. Such facilities are available in only a few hospitals, in particular teaching hospitals with large infertility departments. These tests do not require sophisticated facilities nor are they expensive. They can give a lot more information about the effect your mucus has on your partner's sperm than can post-coital tests and they may save repeated post-coital tests. You may also be given a blood test to see if you have antibodies to sperm.

What do we learn from the post-coital test and other tests of compatibility?
The post-coital test gives information about your cervical mucus and the ability of your partner's sperm to survive in your vagina and pass through the mucus. A poor test may not indicate that you have problems because it may have been badly timed: it is important to have further tests to check this. If the picture is poor after several post-coital tests then you need to consider why this is the case. There may be several reasons.

Is your vagina too acid for the sperm? Sperm cannot survive in a vagina which is too acid. The seminal fluid is alkaline but sometimes it does not compensate sufficiently for the vagina's acidity. Infections and your own body's chemistry may make your vagina too acid, so any infection needs to be treated. Also, there are a number of ways of adjusting your body chemistry. One way is to douche with a mild solution of bicarbonate of soda just prior to intercourse which should reduce acidity temporarily.

For a more permanent effect you could try changing your diet by eating more fruit and vegetables, or use herbs in teas and as douches.[2] It is also worth noting that many lubricants have a spermicidal effect, that is, they kill sperm. If you are trying to get pregnant, or if you go for a post-coital test, you should not use lubricants. If you need some sort of lubrication, you can try using your own saliva.

Can the sperm survive in your cervical mucus? Cervical mucus changes regularly throughout your menstrual cycle but it is the consistency of the mucus just prior to ovulation which is crucial for conception. If your mucus is thin and watery around the middle of the month this is an indication that you have ovulated. However, you may still be ovulating but the balance between the oestrogen and progesterone may not be quite right and so your mucus may remain thick and tacky, trapping the sperm. You may be given oestrogen tablets to improve the quality of mucus, to be taken in the days prior to ovulation. Where clinic sessions do not coincide with your ovulation oestrogen is sometimes prescribed after poor post-coital tests to improve the mucus quality for the next test. Then it is possible to see if the problem lies here or in the low motility of the sperm. In taking oestrogen tablets you may wonder whether you are improving the quality of your mucus to better your chances of conceiving or whether you are improving it to clarify the results of your post-coital test. If you are given Clomid (see p. 82) you may also be given oestrogen tablets to take because the Clomid makes your mucus more tacky.

The other side of the coin here is poor semen; your mucus might be fine but your partner's sperm may be trapped in it. This is confirmed by a semen test or by a cross-hostility test. There are two ways round this problem; either artificial insemination using your partner's semen, or a cervical insemination cap. (We describe these methods in chapter 5.) These same methods are also used when the mucus does not respond to any of the treatments given, as a way of bypassing it.

Do you produce antibodies to your partner's sperm? To protect itself from infections, your body produces antibodies which attack cells recognised as foreign or different from itself. Sometimes it is thought that allergies may develop in this way, by your body reacting to certain harmless substances as if they were harmful. Sperms are foreign to your body and you can develop antibodies to them in the same way as you can develop allergies. In this case a poor post-coital test may be due to your antibodies killing off your partner's sperm. You can have antibodies just in your cervical mucus, but they may also be present in your blood stream.

Two tests are used to locate the antibodies, both tests working on the same principle; one uses cervical mucus and the other a small sample of your blood. In both tests, a sample of fresh semen is introduced and the mix is examined under a microscope. Antibodies cause agglutination, that is, they make the sperm stick together. Agglutination can easily be identified under a microscope. Treatment varies according to the source of your antibodies. If they are in the cervical mucus you are advised to have intercourse with your partner using a condom for about six to nine months. The idea behind this is that your immune system may become less sensitive to sperm and when you have intercourse without using a condom your body is able to tolerate sperm. The effect of this is short-term and the antibodies soon return. Sometimes artificial insemination using your partner's semen and an insemination cap may successfully bypass antibodies. However, you may have antibodies beyond your cervix, in your uterus and Fallopian tubes and these therapies may not be effective. If you have antibodies in your blood, then steroids may be given to suppress their production. Steroids are powerful drugs and should be taken only after weighing up the chances of success against any possible harmful effects.

Whilst compatibility is clearly important for conception, poor compatibility does not mean that you cannot get pregnant, although you may be less likely to do so. Furthermore, there are some treatments available which have a reasonable success rate.

We discuss compatibility as a medical issue, and this is how you will usually see it used in discussions of infertility. But it is also a word that is used to evaluate people's relationships, and occasionally you may feel that the emphasis has moved away from improving the compatibility of mucus and sperm to how compatible you are as people. This may be especially likely to happen when no clear cause of your infertility has been found. In this case it is worth reminding yourself that although you are unable to conceive you can still be successful in other areas and you can still create and sustain good relationships.

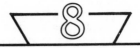

MISCARRIAGE AND
STILLBIRTH

So far, we have focused on infertility caused by an inability to conceive. But conception is only the first step on the road to motherhood. Some women have no children or fewer children than they would like because they cannot carry a pregnancy through to term or give birth to a live infant. Some of these women may have had problems in conceiving so their inability to maintain a pregnancy comes on top of other difficulties. Other women conceive easily enough – their infertility is due to persistent miscarriage.

In medical terms, the loss of a pregnancy before the twenty-eighth week is known as a spontaneous abortion; we prefer to use the non-medical term, miscarriage. After about the twenty-eighth week, a premature ending of a pregnancy is known as a pre-term delivery and there is a fairly good chance of the baby surviving. If the baby dies after the twenty-eighth week, either in the uterus or soon after delivery, it is called a stillbirth.

There are a number of medical terms used to describe a fertilised egg as it develops. Two are used most frequently: once a pregnancy is established and up to the twelfth week, the egg is termed an embryo; after the twelfth week, a foetus. The terms distinguish the different kinds of development that are taking place. During the embryonic period, most of the internal and external structure of the body takes shape; during the foetal period, the body grows and matures until it is able to function outside its mother's body. The terms also indicate the different threats during pregnancy. However, to avoid a proliferation of medical terms, we use the term foetus alone to describe the developing organism at all stages of pregnancy.

MISCARRIAGE

Miscarriage is not an uncommon event. About three out of ten conceptions result in a live birth, or put another way, as many as seven out of ten do not.[1] This number looks very high but it is important to remember that eight out of ten of these miscarriages (six out of ten conceptions) occur in the first two weeks of pregnancy when the fertilised egg fails to implant itself into the uterus. This sort of miscarriage happens before the woman is aware that she is pregnant; the only sign of her lost pregnancy might be a heavy period. Once the fertilised egg establishes itself in the wall of the uterus, a miscarriage is unlikely to go unnoticed and it is the experience of these miscarriages that we discuss.

What happens when you have a miscarriage
The first signs of a miscarriage are bleeding and cramps. Initially, blood loss may be slight, no more than spotting. You may experience cramps, sometimes quite severe, not unlike a mini-labour. If the placenta remains attached to the wall of the uterus, you may escape with only a threatened miscarriage and you will not lose the baby. This can happen even when quite a lot of blood is lost.

I didn't feel too good and then I started to miscarry. I went to hospital because I had started to bleed and they made me lie flat on my back for a week. I couldn't believe it, one minute I was working and the next minute I was flat on my back. I couldn't even go to the lavatory, I couldn't get out of bed. That was all the treatment entailed. From then on I had to stop work immediately. I had a home help and I couldn't do much myself.

Once the placenta separates itself from the wall of the uterus, the pregnancy cannot continue. In *Why Children?* Melba Wilson describes her experience.[2]

About two months into my pregnancy, I started to miscarry. It was the day before New Year's Eve and I was so scared I was sick, more from worry than from the actual miscarriage. From my reading, I knew there was a chance I could stop it if I got into bed immediately, which I did. I phoned the doctor, told him what was happening and he said I'd done exactly the right thing and I was under no circumstances to attempt to get up. I was in bed for the next three days, and still the bleeding didn't stop. I was eventually taken to hospital for more bed rest – and I still bled. After three days, during which time they'd done tests to try and detect a foetal heartbeat (and found none), the bleeding had increased and was now coming out in big clots. I prayed and prayed that the inevitable wouldn't happen. But it did.

On the fourth day in hospital they told me they would have to do a D & C on me in order to get the rest of the aborted foetus out.

The placenta may expel itself but sometimes some of the foetal and placental material remain in the uterus. In this case, it is necessary to have a D & C (dilation and curettage, a minor operation) to clear the contents of the uterus after which the uterus can begin to heal. As the uterine lining heals, you may bleed slightly. Heavier bleeding may indicate that not all the contents of the uterus have been cleared and you may require further medical attention, so do not hesitate to contact your doctor.

Sometimes the foetus dies in the uterus where it can remain for some time. In such cases, the symptoms are the disappearance of the signs of pregnancy. The foetus may then be lost naturally, by the woman going into labour, or it may have to be removed. This is done either with a D & C or by inducing labour, depending how far advanced the pregnancy is when the foetus dies.

Although I had lost it at ten weeks, I don't think it had ever really got going. I felt very pregnant for about three weeks, different from how I'd ever felt before. But then I lost those symptoms and all I felt was a dull ache. I think whatever was there was dead, but I just didn't lose it.

You may lose quickly the symptoms of pregnancy but it can take several months for your menstrual cycle to return to normal and during that time the discomfort or the bleeding may persist. And although it has ended, your pregnancy is not forgotten easily.

I felt sorry for me when it came to it. One day I had a baby growing inside me and the next I didn't. My breasts, which had grown bigger and were the only outward sign of my pregnancy, quickly went back to their normal size. It's hard to describe the sense of devastation and loss I felt.

To lose a baby through a miscarriage is an unpleasant, debilitating physical experience, but it is also an emotional shock; few women anticipate losing a pregnancy.

Miscarriage never entered the scheme of things as far as I was concerned. I never dreamed of miscarriage. It wasn't until later that I discovered how common it is.

A miscarriage is a loss; it is the loss of a child which you conceived and which you expected to deliver. And so it is only natural for you to feel the need to grieve this loss.

The miscarriage was also a bereavement, in the real sense of the word. I'm approaching the time when it would have been due, and as that gets closer, I get more and more sad and depressed about it.

The causes of miscarriage
What causes a miscarriage? We do know some of the reasons why women miscarry, although there are still many questions about pregnancy for which there are no good answers. However, when it comes to asking why you miscarried and whether you are likely to do so when you get pregnant again, then you may not get any clear answer. One reason for this is that as most women who miscarry go on to give birth without further problems, it is unusual for hospitals to try to establish the cause of a first miscarriage. Sometimes, women have to miscarry three times before being labelled a 'habitual aborter' and given tests. If you retain any bits of matter you lose during a miscarriage, you may be able to have

tests carried out sooner. Many women are quite disturbed when their miscarriage is not investigated and that what is a difficult emotional experience for them is treated medically with such lack of concern.

The causes of miscarriage can be grouped roughly into three types; genetic, developmental problems, and disorders of the mother's reproductive system. About seven out of eight miscarriages occur in the first twelve weeks of pregnancy, during the embryonic period. These early miscarriages are thought usually to be associated with different factors from those of later miscarriages, so the point in your pregnancy at which you miscarry may offer some clues as to the cause.

Genetic factors: Genetic factors are the most common cause of early miscarriage, that is miscarriage during the first twelve weeks of pregnancy. Most genetic abnormalities occur by chance at fertilisation when the genes of the egg and sperm mix. Such an abnormality may prevent the cells from dividing properly so the fertilised egg fails to implant in the uterus. When the fertilised egg fails to survive, the term often used is 'blighted ovum' implying that the egg's genetic material is at fault. This can make the woman feel very guilty that her genetic deficiencies are causing the miscarriage. But of course the foetus is a mixture of her own and the father's genetic material, and it is rarely possible to say at this stage which material came from which parent.

Sometimes a foetus with genetic abnormalities survives this stage either to be miscarried later in the pregnancy or to be born as a baby with congenital abnormalities. Some of these abnormalities can be detected during pregnancy with foetal monitoring devices. (These techniques are discussed more fully in chapter 9.) About two in every hundred live births result in a baby who is disabled in some way, the majority not severely.

Miscarriages caused by genetic abnormalities usually occur at random and so are unlikely in any subsequent pregnancy. In very rare cases, the mother or the father has a genetic problem which is likely to recur. There is no treatment available to modify such genetic abnormalities prior to birth. So if you are one of the small number of women who miscarry repeatedly in the first twelve weeks of pregnancy then you should try to obtain genetic testing and counselling.

Developmental problems: Very occasionally, a fertilised egg which is perfectly normal at conception suffers damage in the uterus. The placenta usually acts as a very efficient filter and prevents harmful substances from the mother's body reaching the foetus. However, some harmful substances, called teratogens, can cross from the mother's body through the placenta and damage the developing foetus. These substances include radiation from X-rays, certain viruses such as syphilis and German measles, nicotine and alcohol, some chemicals and metals and certain drugs, the most notorious of which is thalidomide. The nature and extent of the damage such substances cause depends in part on when during a pregnancy the foetus is exposed. For instance, there is clear evidence that if the foetus is exposed to the German measles virus in the first twelve weeks of pregnancy, there is a significant risk of its hearing being damaged. But exposure to the virus later in pregnancy does not carry the same risks. It is when the organs are forming and taking shape that they are most vulnerable to deformity. A damaged foetus is more likely to be miscarried. Later in the pregnancy when the foetus is growing and maturing, the effect of such harmful substances is to slow down its growth. Recent studies have suggested that nicotine and alcohol can depress the function of the placenta, reducing the supply of oxygen to the foetus. Sometimes, the mother's own health, her diet and environment can lead to a poorly nourished foetus, probably because the placenta is inadequate. Retarded foetal growth may mean a more sickly baby whose chances of survival are reduced, and a greater risk of stillbirth or death in the first few days of a baby's life. Such misfortunes are more common amongst women of lower socio-economic background where the mother's diet and environment are poor. Incidences of stillbirth and early death are used as indicators of a country's overall standard of living.

Because the foetus is most vulnerable in the early weeks – perhaps before you know that you are pregnant – the only way you can deal with teratogens is to avoid them. Women planning to be pregnant should make sure that they are immunised against German measles. But some of these hazards might relate to employment. If you notice that other women at your place of employment have frequent miscarriages, you may want to find out whether any of the production processes are harmful to the foetus. The Women and Work Hazards Group can be of assistance here. But clearly there are limits to what you can do yourself; you cannot always control your work environment, your housing or your diet. And many teratogenic agents are still to be detected. Fortunately, the risk of severe damage to the foetus during its development is small, thanks largely to the efficiency of the placenta.

Disorders of the woman's reproductive system: To survive and grow, the foetus requires protection and nourishment from the mother's body. The placenta sustains the foetus with nourishment and oxygen and filters out harmful substances. The uterus gives physical protection, expanding to provide the growing foetus with room to develop and then pushing the foetus out when – and only when – it is able to survive independently of its mother's body. During pregnancy, the mother's menstrual cycle is suppressed; her hormones are active elsewhere – for example, in instructing the breasts to produce milk or in triggering the contractions of the uterus which expel the foetus into the world. Should any of these processes go wrong, then a pregnancy can be put at risk. Unfortunately, these processes are as yet poorly understood and there is little in the way of routine treatment.

Most miscarriages occur between eight and twelve weeks of pregnancy. It has been suggested that some women do not produce enough progesterone at the beginning of pregnancy to suppress completely their menstrual cycle with the result that the pregnancy is lost. Giving women progesterone early on in pregnancy has not proved successful and, in any case, doctors are becoming more cautious about prescribing drugs during pregnancy because of possible damage to the foetus. Sometimes an attempt is made to boost the amount of progesterone produced by the ovaries in the cycle in which a woman conceives by prescribing Clomid (see chapter 5).

Another idea is that the foetus is rejected by the mother's immune system. The immune system recognises and rejects foreign bodies including germs and viruses; it is this system which has to be suppressed in organ transplant to prevent rejection. The foetus is made up of genetic material from its father as well as its mother and technically, it is foreign to its mother's own body chemistry. It is puzzling that the uterus accepts such foreign material. In the majority of cases, the fertilised egg is accepted, but perhaps in some rare cases, the mother's immune system is especially sensitive and rejects a foetus.

Certain illnesses, such as diabetes, kidney disease and high blood pressure can lead to problems in maintaining a pregnancy. Women with these disorders should be monitored carefully.

Abnormalities of the uterus such as fibroids, or an unusual shape, or a weakened cervix, can cause miscarriage. By and large, these are responsible for miscarriages in the later part of a pregnancy, after the fourteenth week.

Fibroids or myomas are benign (non-cancerous) tumours of the uterus. (We also discuss fibroids in chapter 6.) Fibroids can prevent conception, but perhaps more importantly, they can interfere with a pregnancy. They can do this either because the fertilised egg implants itself on a fibroid where the blood supply is insufficient to maintain the growth of the foetus, or because the fibroid itself grows during pregnancy, not leaving enough space in the uterus for the growing foetus. Women with fibroids frequently do bear children and fibroids are only rarely a problem although they are removed sometimes to maximise the chances of a successful pregnancy.

Some women are born with a uterus of an unusual shape;[3] it may be divided completely or partially into two with a wall (septum) separating the two parts, or it may have only one horn. An unusually shaped uterus is not a bar to a succesful pregnancy but it can make one difficult. Some women miscarry either because the fertilised egg implants itself on the septum where it is unable to obtain sufficient nourishment or because the part of the uterus containing the foetus is unable to stretch and accommodate the growing foetus.

For reasons that are not at all well understood, the cervix is sometimes unable to cope with the increasing weight and pressure of the foetus in the uterus and dilates (opens) so that the foetus is lost prematurely. A difficult birth or inept medical manipulation may leave the cervix weakened. A dilated cervix may be observed at an internal examination, in which case it is labelled 'incompetent', an unfortunate term because it seems to pass judgement on the ability of a woman to carry a pregnancy. Sometimes a stitch is put in the cervix to prevent the loss of the pregnancy: it is removed just prior to birth. But the main kind of treatment offered is bed rest. Women are told to lie still for days, weeks or months, sometimes confined to hospital in the hope that the pressure on the cervix is relieved.

Non-medical causes of miscarriage: We have outlined most of the suggested medical causes of miscarriage. Many of these are only hypothetical as there is very little good scientific evidence to support them. Miscarriage is not an area in which a great deal of research is being conducted and so very often you cannot be told with any degree of certainty why you miscarried. However, many other ideas are put forward about the causes of miscarriage for which there is even less good evidence. These include doing too much exercise, going on a long trip, working too hard, or having sexual intercourse. In fact, once a foetus is implanted firmly in the uterus, it is very difficult to dislodge and it can, in fact, survive considerable shock. As one women points out,

> My dear mother who's in her eighties now would go out and scrub floors in the local convent for the nuns half the night and would come back with her knees bleeding and yet she was still able to produce healthy, live children.

What seems to happen is that other people, or even the woman herself, look back over her life immediately before she had the miscarriage and seize upon some incident as the cause so that if she went swimming the day before the miscarriage, then the swim must be the cause. This is faulty logic; it is wrong to assume that just because one event preceded another it was the cause. Most women engage in physical exercise, in sexual activity and in work without putting their pregnancies at risk. If these activities are associated with miscarriage, we need to know why the majority of women do not miscarry most of the time.

Sometimes emotional as well as physical factors are said to cause a miscarriage. Your body may physically reject a foetus but it does not mean that it is emotionally rejected. We can find ample proof that our minds do not have such clear control over our bodies when we look at the number of women who have unwanted pregnancies.

Bed rest: When a miscarriage threatens, bed rest is the main form of treatment offered: its effectiveness is at best equivocal. Whilst it can certainly do no harm to take to your bed for a few days or weeks during pregnancy, it is no guarantee of a successful outcome. Some women are willing to try this remedy and to remain bedridden for weeks or months in the hope of keeping a pregnancy. For other women, the sacrifice of a job and normal social contact for months is too difficult, especially when the effectiveness of the treatment is itself in doubt. Ultimately, only you can make that choice.

> When they turned round to me and said, wrap yourself up in cotton wool, otherwise that's it, I thought it was a bit under the belt. To present you with a choice of a job or a baby is a bit much.

If a woman does go on to miscarry, then the support and consolation of her friends and the distraction of her work can be very important. Isolating her early on in her pregnancy may deny her these powerful sources of comfort.

Like ideas about the causes of miscarriage, many of those about bed rest as treatment are based on faulty logic. So, for instance, if a woman takes to her bed as soon as a miscarriage threatens and the miscarriage is averted, then it is assumed that bed rest worked as a cure.

We feel that double standards operate when doctors and experts on childbirth talk about pregnancy and physical activity. On the one hand, pregnant women are encouraged to be active, to exercise and to continue to have sexual relations. But once a miscarriage threatens, we find that all activity is labelled dangerous and is said to dislodge the foetus. It is little wonder that women become confused.

Unless you miscarry frequently, there is little available in the way of investigation, nor is there much in the way of successful treatment. We have all learnt to rely on medical help and so it can be unnerving to discover this. It seems to imply, too, that miscarriage is of little consequence, but clearly it matters to you, in the short term because of the emotional and physical shock, and in the long term because of worries about subsequent pregnancies and perhaps because your family will be smaller than you intended. Fortunately, as we have said, most women who miscarry go on to have successful pregnancies. Those women who miscarry persistently may find chapters 9 and 10 useful.

STILLBIRTH

After twenty eight weeks of pregnancy, the death of a foetus is called a stillbirth whether it dies in the uterus or during labour. Stillbirth today is a fairly unusual event; there are about eight stillbirths for every one thousand live births in the United Kingdom, and another eight babies die in the first days after birth (perinatal death).

What happens when you have a stillbirth? Sometimes a woman becomes aware that the foetus has stopped moving about and wonders whether something has gone amiss.

The kicking was less vigorous and then it stopped altogether. I totally panicked. I kept telling myself that the baby was just resting up before delivery or that she was saving all her energy for the final growth spurt. But I knew deep down that something was wrong.

At other times, the first warning that something has gone wrong may be when medical staff are unable to hear the foetal heartbeat at a routine test, during labour or shortly after birth.

My labour was going along fine but then, when the nurse checked the baby's heartbeat, she didn't hear anything... And then she left the room. I wasn't worried. Sometimes my doctor during previous prenatal examinations had had trouble finding the heartbeat. They rushed me to the labour room and attached another foetal heart monitor. There was still no sign of a heartbeat. I knew something was wrong. The doctor said, sadly we're expecting the worst.[4]

A woman who has a stillbirth goes through the business of childbirth – all the preparations, hospitalisation and delivery. Sometimes, a stillborn baby is induced but some mothers have to wait to go into labour normally, fairly certain that the foetus inside them has died. If there is thought to be any doubt about the safety of the foetus or the mother's health, the baby will be delivered by Caesarean section. Many hospitals try to ensure that a woman who has a stillbirth is kept away from wards full of mothers, usually by giving her a room of her own. Privacy is clearly important.

Today, mothers of stillborn babies are encouraged to see their dead child to give them a concrete person over which to grieve.

> I didn't see my baby unfortunately. It happened before it was as common as it is today. I wasn't encouraged to do so. No one said, we think you should see the baby so you know it's the baby you lost. When you have another baby, you won't get them confused in your head; so you won't go dashing along to the nursery and kidnap a couple. These things do happen.

Seeing the baby helps to allay any worries or fantasies mothers may have about their babies. 'We looked carefully at all his features, and then we returned him quickly to the nurse. But I'll always remember how he looked, he was beautiful, not at all like the monster I was expecting to see.' Mothers of congenitally abnormal babies are sometimes pleased to know that despite its disabilities, the baby had a beauty of its own.

Hospital staff sometimes describe the appearance of a stillborn baby as macerated; this unpleasant term is the medical word used to describe the wrinkled appearance of some stillborn babies, like skin that has been in water for some time.

No one can tell you how long it will take you to accept the reality of your loss and to mourn your dead child; some women take longer than others. Parents of stillborn babies are encouraged to name the child, to give it a proper burial. For legal reasons, stillborn babies have a post-mortem. Although these are painful procedures for parents to go through, they are further recognition of your loss of an individual child.[5]

Because it is nowadays unusual for babies to die in childbirth, we expect it always to be a happy time. Being the mother of a stillborn baby or knowing someone whose baby has died breaks with all our expectations and makes our usual ways of coping quite inappropriate. One moment you are all geared up for happiness, the next moment you need to mourn and grieve.

What are the causes of stillbirth? There are two main causes: congenital abnormalities and placental malfunctioning or insufficiency, the second being the most common. For reasons which are not well understood, the placenta stops working altogether or ceases to function properly and so fails to nourish the foetus. The chances of losing another child through stillbirth are small; once the body has produced one placenta, it appears to get better at doing it. And if the placenta failed because it was awkwardly placed (placenta praevia), then the chances of a similar problem arising in subsequent pregnancies is very small. Unfortunately, the risks of another placenta failure are the same in subsequent pregnancies where malnourishment or disease have reduced the general health of the mother.

The other main cause of stillbirth, congenital abnormalities – that is abnormalities caused both by genetic disorders and by damage to the foetus as it develops – we have discussed in detail in the previous section on the causes of miscarriage. Spina bifida is the most commonly cited congenital abnormality which leads to stillbirth. And sadly, there is quite a high chance of any subsequent pregnancies having the same problem. If this is your situation, then you may be offered genetic counselling.

HAVING A BABY AFTER A MISCARRIAGE OR STILLBIRTH

Friends or medical people may suggest that it would help you to forget about the miscarriage or the child you've have lost if you go ahead quickly with another pregnancy. Discussions in books about how long you should wait before you try to get pregnant again is limited largely to recovering physically. Because such advice ignores women's feeling about their loss, it can be difficult and sometimes even unhelpful advice to follow. The idea that one pregnancy can replace or compensate for an earlier lost one seems to deny the reality of the loss. Each conception and pregnancy is experienced individually; one cannot readily replace another. Such advice is a denial of your grief, of the need to mourn, and it can be painful even when you want to get pregnant and feel confident that you will be able to do so. 'Even though I knew I would get pregnant again, I was not comforted. *This* baby, my first baby, was not to be.'

Having a miscarriage or a stillbirth alters the way you feel about your next pregnancy; you will probably feel more anxious than a woman without your history.

After I heard the test was positive, I became tearful and worried. I didn't know what to do. I just wanted to stay in bed. I became obsessed with my body. I still don't believe that I'm not going to bleed any minute. I'm fully expecting it to happen. And I think to myself, I'll be glad when it does happen because then I'll be out of my misery.

Surprisingly, this is a topic rarely discussed in any of the books on pregnancy and childbirth. Instead, it is assumed that once pregnant, you forget any previous negative experiences. But although at some point in your pregnancy and childrearing, your experience of miscarriage or stillbirth fades and motherhood predominates, the moment at which this happens varies for each woman. Your anxiety may persist through more than one pregnancy.

I got pregnant again only four months after I lost the first one. It was earlier than I planned and I considered an abortion because I felt I wasn't ready for it yet. I got very depressed during the pregnancy. Feeling fatalistic, if it works or if it doesn't. With my next pregnancy, it was different. Every second Friday night I'd have hysterics; two weeks was as long as I could cope. With the first pregnancy I was more accepting but I was anxious.

Much attention has been given to the ways in which childbirth is conducted. Groups such as the National Childbirth Trust are actively involved in helping women to understand what is involved in childbirth and try to ensure that women are able to have the kind of birth they would like, often natural and non-technological. But women who have had miscarriages or a stillbirth often feel unsure about the way in which they want their childbirth managed and may feel gratitude towards the doctor who has helped them. Some women welcome all the medical technology and see it as comforting insurance and feel angry at the implication that they have been brainwashed or that they are depriving themselves of a life-enhancing experience.

I was plugged into all the machines. I went on to the foetal heart monitor every day. I knew that my baby was still alive, that if there was the least sign of anything going wrong, everybody was there to do something about it immediately. I wasn't at home thinking, 'It's not kicking as much as it was.'

Other women may feel that because of the negative experience of miscarriage or stillbirth they want their childbirth experience to be especially good. A good and happy delivery is a worthwhile goal for every woman, and a woman's views about what she wants for her delivery should be heard. Being able to see, to hold or to feed a baby in the moments after birth, especially when loved ones are present to share the experience, arouses powerful feelings in everyone. It is an opportunity which should be available to as many mothers as possible. Increasingly, however, it is being suggested that a woman's, and more latterly a man's, relationship with a baby can develop only if they have this opportunity to get to know the baby. It is sad that what a woman may want for herself can only be justified or argued for in terms of what can be seen to be good for her child, reinforcing the view of women as only vessels for their children. Furthermore, there is no good evidence to suggest that a happy delivery or immediate contact with a baby are in themselves necessary for this relationship to develop. Many of us who did not have this experience have developed good strong relationships with our mothers and fathers.[6] Ultimately it is the relationship with a child which is important rather than how the child was delivered.

My third delivery was dreadful. I thought my body had been used and proved to work, it would be easy. It wasn't. It came as a big shock. But because of the stillbirth I'd developed a more realistic attitude. I wasn't so disappointed with myself. You don't have to have a beautiful birth experience in order to have a beautiful relationship with your child; similarly you don't automatically have a beautiful relationship with your child if you've had a beautiful birth experience.

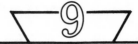

BECOMING A MOTHER: PREGNANCY, ADOPTION, FOSTERING AND SHARED CHILDCARE

About two out of every three women who go through infertility investigation eventually become mothers. Many conceive and bear children, others become mothers by adoption or by fostering children. In this chapter, we look at these routes to motherhood.

PREGNANCY AND CHILDBEARING EXPERIENCES OF INFERTILE WOMEN

Women who have been through infertility investigations often react differently to their pregnancies, to their childbirth and to their childrearing. Finding out that you are pregnant, that at last your period has not come, is a time of elation and excitement. But pregnancy can activate or reactivate doubts and anxieties which, in your effort to become pregnant, you had put aside. Many of these doubts are experienced by all women approaching motherhood, but the experience of infertility can heighten anxieties; will all that effort prove worthwhile? When it has taken so long to conceive a child, you may think that you should feel nothing but unadulterated joy and love. But after spending months or years trying to get pregnant, it is very likely that you have built up very unrealistic expectations about the joys of motherhood, and what your child will be like, expectations which any child would find difficulty in fulfilling.

> I did say to my mother, what if I had a really shitty kid? A nasty horrible child. What if it's got something wrong with it? You'd think I went to all that effort and struggle and now look at this horrid child I've got at the end of it. Your expectations for this child would be so much higher because you'd suffered so much. What if you actually don't enjoy being a parent? She said you always have to assume you are going to enjoy it. You always take that risk.

Some women conceive long after they have given up all hope, after going a long way to resolve their infertility, by adopting children or by finding a new direction for their lives. For them, pregnancy may come at a bad time, or too late in the day.

> It's funny because when I got pregnant everyone expected me to be delighted. But I felt cheated, as if she had arrived too late. I had

so convinced myself that I didn't want a baby, that I couldn't work up any enthusiasm. People used to say, oh you must be thrilled, but I wasn't. By that time I was fearful about what the effects would be on my relationship with my adopted children. Everyone was so pleased for me, but I wasn't thrilled a bit.

Infertile women have a long time to think about motherhood and the kinds of mothers they would make; often they have expectations which no one could hope to live up to. Feeling that your child is such a very special gift may make you think that you should be prepared to sacrifice everything for it.

I suppose I've always felt slightly guilty as a mother, maybe because it was difficult to conceive. Maybe then you feel you've got to be eternally grateful and happy because you've done it. And I find it hard being a mother at times. I feel guilty because I am not a good mother.

Because of the experience of infertility you may feel that your relationship with your child is different, perhaps more intense.

I'm not as casual about her as some mothers are with their children. Every morning I make a bit of a song and a dance about seeing her again. And I know other people don't do that. They just get the child and get it ready, loving them in their own way. But I have to demonstrate it the whole time.

Most babies are precious and most mothers feel ambivalent about them, at least some of the time. All children can be frustrating and disappointing, and the quality of your relationship does not depend on children being lovable all the time. All mothers feel overwhelmed at times and wish there was more space for them, and most mothers, unfortunately, feel guilty about such ideas. Mothers who have taken longer to bear children are articulating fears and worries that all mothers feel. Your reactions and the ways in which you deal with them are similar to those of other mothers. Your personality and the strategies you have developed in coping are probably much more important ultimately than the fact that you took a long time to conceive.

Your experience of infertility shapes the physical process of pregnancy and childbirth. Because it has been difficult for you to conceive, you may feel that there are bound to be problems with your pregnancy or with your child.

I had a trouble-free pregnancy. The first three months of the pregnancy though were agony. I was terrified that something would go wrong. Everyone goes through that, I think, but perhaps we were more aware of it. You feel like you've got much more invested in it.

Women who conceive after a long course of investigations are likely to be older than women who conceive without medical help. As older women and especially as first-time older mothers (elderly primigravida), you are considered to be at risk of complications – such as high blood pressure and the emergence of latent diabetes – during pregnancy; you are more likely to miscarry; to have a longer labour; to give birth to a Down's syndrome child; and to die during childbirth.[1] The risks are higher for older women, but they must be seen in perspective. A woman aged 35 to 39 is three and one half times more likely to die in childbirth than a woman aged between 20 and 24. But the maternal mortality rate is fortunately very low at all ages, so put another way, the chances of dying in childbirth at age 20 to 24 are one in 6800 and, at 35 to 39, are still low at one in 1950. These figures are further complicated by the issue of social class, so that just being older is not in itself so important. The risk of giving birth to a Down's syndrome baby also increases with age; you are five times more likely to give birth to a Down's syndrome baby if you are aged 35 to 40 than if you are aged 25 to 30. The risks increase from one in 1500 babies to one in 300, although because most babies are born to younger women more Down's syndrome children are born to younger mothers.

Because there are these risks any older woman, and especially an older primigravida, is monitored more carefully during pregnancy. She is probably given an ultrasonic scan to check the foetus' development, whether she is expecting more than one baby and the position of the placenta. Scans are often used to check the age of the foetus, although most women undergoing infertility investigations are probably very aware of their cycles and when they conceived. It is important that all women who take ovulation-inducing drugs should be given an ultrasonic scan because there is a higher risk of multiple pregnancies with this treatment. Twin pregnancies and deliveries are generally more complicated and hence involve more medical supervision, and twins are more likely to go into special care baby units than are singletons.[2]

Older pregnant women are now being given amniocentesis more routinely. Amniocentesis examines foetal cells for abnormalities. It is performed at 16 to 18 weeks of pregnancy. You are given a local anaesthetic and then a fine needle is inserted into your uterus and a sample of the fluid in the sac surrounding the foetus is drawn off. This fluid is taken away for examination for genetic abnormalities such as spina bifida and Down's syndrome. Because the test involves some slight interference with the foetus there is a small risk of miscarriage. If the test indicates a problem, you have to decide whether or not to abort. Many hospitals assume that you will abort if anything is found to be wrong. However, this may not be an easy decision for you to make.[3] You may be anxious about how much you could love and care for a handicapped child and, after all your efforts to conceive, how you could cope with a child that was less than perfect. But you may feel that, despite these worries, you do not want to give up on a much wanted pregnancy and a much wanted child. After working so hard you are ready to accept a child, whatever its problems. Given the negative view our society, and often we ourselves, have of disability, this is an extremely difficult decision to make. There may be pressure from medical staff, from friends and relatives to make the 'sensible' decision. We believe that women should have an opportunity to talk to other people, especially to the parents of disabled children, about what bringing up a disabled child can be like before they are forced to make a decision.

So, because of your increased age and your infertility experiences, there may be some aspects of your pregnancy which are different. These are reflected in the ways in which you approach your pregnancy.

> I always wanted to carry on working, even reduced hours. I would put the child in a nursery. But now after five years trying to get pregnant I decided to give up work for a while. It's changed my attitude. I was very adamant that women should not disrupt their lives but now the benefits of actually watching my child grow up have loomed so large that I think I will stay at home.

Your experience of infertility affects the way in which you react to the ante-natal treatment you receive. Pregnancy may transfer you from a hospital's infertility clinic to the ante-natal clinic, and your care may be overseen by the same consultant.

> I was very lucky because at the ante-natal clinic I saw the doctor who had begun my infertility treatment. I think it helped being an interesting case. They paid more attention to things and I saw fewer doctors.

Once delivered, your baby is treated as 'precious'.

> Women who had attended the infertility clinic got the 'precious' tag attached to their babies. I was always treated very nicely.

Your long medical encounter during your infertility investigations may have desensitised you to medical technology and manipulation, and the impersonality of ante-natal care or the unpleasantness of frequent internal examinations may seem less shocking. Generally too there is an increase in pressure on women to see pregnancy as problematic and needing continuous medical supervision. Some women are so grateful to be having a child that they may feel that they have lost the right to demand a different kind of treatment. That you are pregnant, that you have a child may be all that matters to you.

> I was as high as a kite. I had to have a Caesarian. The pain was nothing. I just grinned from ear to ear, morning until night. Nothing would stop me. I'd be staggering up the ward, wincing, but grinning all the time. I was one of the lucky ones that falls in love with her baby at first sight. I did think she was absolutely wonderful, marvellous. She was such a shock to me. I couldn't believe my luck that she was a girl and that there was nothing wrong with her.

There is a good deal of stress on the naturalness of pregnancy. Women who have gone to elaborate procedures to get pregnant may feel, however, that there is little that is natural about their conceptions and so find it hard to identify with this emphasis in much of what is written about pregnancy. As we said in chapter 8, books written for pregnant women tend to ignore women's fertility histories – this is a great shame.

Women who take a long time to conceive are more at risk of miscarrying. It is not clear why this should be the case; perhaps the hormonal problems which make conception difficult for some women also make it more difficult to maintain a pregnancy. The risks of miscarriage are also higher in older women, and clearly the longer you take to get pregnant the older you will be when you are pregnant. Infertile women often fear miscarriage even if they have not experienced it themselves. Having problems in conceiving has made them more thoughtful or more aware of other reproductive hazards. You may feel ambivalent about miscarriage; on the one hand at least you have demonstrated your ability to conceive, you have had the experience of being pregnant even if for only a short time.

> After a year of trying I conceived. It was an extraordinarily exciting experience, not just that I had conceived, but I found being pregnant exciting too. I got as far as ten weeks. It was worth it even if I never got pregnant again, it was worth having the experience.

On the other hand to have got so far and yet still be without a child is very hard. Discussions about whether to wait for some time before trying to conceive again seem very academic to a woman who has spent years achieving a first pregnancy and whose one and only pregnancy might be unsuccessful.

> When I'd met a woman who'd had a miscarriage, I used to think, they're lucky, at least they've been pregnant, at least they've had the thrill of being able to do that. But everyone seemed to think it was worse. Then when I was pregnant on one occasion I thought I was going to lose her. I was pretty desperate. It would have been a lot worse. You get yourself all geared up, over the moon because you're pregnant.

For the infertile woman getting pregnant again may mean another long wait, perhaps a return to the infertility clinic for further treatment or having to start AID all over again. Just as that part of your life seemed behind you, you are faced with the decision about whether to persist and seek further treatment.

ADOPTION

The idea behind adoption is that a child not born to you is brought into your family and treated as your child; a legally adopted child has the same rights as a natural child. Many infertile people and the professionals they meet believe that adopting a child provides a solution to childlessness. Unfortunately the chances of an infertile person adopting a child are not high, nor is it an easy or acceptable solution for all infertile people.

In practical terms your chances of adopting a baby are slim. After the Second World War adoptions increased, reaching a maximum of nearly 25,000 in 1966.[4] Since then the number of children adopted each year has fallen, so that by 1980 only 10,600 children were adopted. And in fact the number of babies adopted by infertile couples has fallen more dramatically than the overall figures suggest. In 1980 only 954 infants under the age of six months were adopted. Set against an estimate of 40,000 new cases of infertility each year, it becomes clear that adopting a baby is no longer an easy solution. There are a number of reasons for this baby shortage. The greater availability of contraception to young and unmarried women and of legalised abortions since 1967 coincided with much more tolerant attitudes towards illegitimacy. Most women now keep the babies they deliver, whether they are married or not, leaving fewer babies available for adoption.

That leaves 9,700 older children adopted in 1980, but few of these were adopted by infertile people. Reforms in the divorce laws has made second marriages more common and many children are being adopted by step-parents. These children account for a large number of older children adopted. As adoption has become a more acceptable practice many other parents are choosing to increase their family by adopting babies or older children.

So the picture that many of us have, and that includes many professionals, is out of date. The time when it was easy to adopt has long since passed. 'His aunt adopted two children. She's in her sixties now. She went to the children's home and chose a little boy. But he wouldn't go without his friend so they took him as well.'

The policy of adoption agencies has also changed; they now see themselves as more concerned with finding what *they* consider to be good homes for their children rather than trying to provide a service for infertile people. Many agencies prefer to place a child and especially an older, or a disabled child, or a group of brothers and sisters with people who have proved their parenting skills by bringing up their own children. For infertile people it means that adoption is no longer an easy – or indeed for many – a possible way of building a family.

Adoption gives you a child but you cannot thereby escape coming to terms with your inability to bear a child of your own. Adoption societies recognise this and talk about the need for you to work through your infertility before applying for adoption. In their booklet 'Adopting a child', the British Agencies for Adoption and Fostering say, 'You may need time to get over the shock if you have just learned that you are unlikely to have a child born to you.' As neither they, nor the infertility clinics themselves, with very few exceptions, offer any counselling you are probably thrown back very much on your own resources in trying to come to terms with your infertility.

Deciding to adopt a child

For some women the decision to try to adopt is made easily and quickly; perhaps they are less concerned with the biological aspects of motherhood and from the beginning they feel that adoption is a satisfactory alternative. In this case, it is possible to run adoption procedures alongside their infertility investigations.

> We started the adoption ball rolling at the same time as the infertility investigations. It did take the tension off it. I'm sure we were no more uptight than other people going through it. In fact, running it in parallel was a great help. When things were going badly with the doctor it was a great help to know it wasn't our only hope. In fact, once we were accepted on to the adoption list, I didn't feel any need to go on with the infertility.

Other women feel equally clearly that adoption is not a satisfactory solution, one they never feel able to consider. For them any discussion of adoption arouses a sense of failure. This was the reaction of Liz in *Daughters of Jerusalem*:

> Two years ago Ian had been seized with an enthusiasm to adopt a Cambodian war-orphan, which he was convinced were readily available... She had been furious with him for giving up hope in her, for expressing even by implication the idea that they would not have a child of their own, for pretending that such a substitution could be the real thing, for not understanding that the craving was in her gut and that craving could only be alleviated there.[5]

The decision to try to adopt may only be reached when conception is ruled out. While there is still hope that the investigations might succeed, women are reluctant to invest their energies in adoption. But ideas change with time; as infertility investigations proceed, alternatives which would have been dismissed without question in the early days come to seem possible and even attractive.

Whatever your feelings about adoption, you may fear the intrusive nature of the procedures coming on top of the infertility investigations and that may influence your decision about when or whether to try for adoption. But it is worth remembering that it can take time to persuade an adoption agency to consider your case, and even longer to get a child, if you get one at all. Agencies do have age limits. If you are in your late thirties you may be considered too old, or if you have been married for many years, you may be thought to have become too stuck in your ways and so not such good prospective parents. So your needs to set your own pace have to be tempered by such constraints.

What does the decision to adopt involve? Clearly, it is shaped by a whole range of factors such as what having a child means to you and the reactions and feelings of those around you. These in turn are affected by your experiences of infertility. We look at some of these issues.

Being pregnant and giving birth

Adopting a child means that you miss out on being pregnant and giving birth to that child. Your relationship starts at a different point in his or her life and through a different route. For some women pregnancy and childbirth are just the necessary means to motherhood; it is a child they want and for them it is less important how they become mothers. These women stress the emotional bond, their relationship with the child as the vital link and express less concern with the biological ties. 'I feel that my adopted children are my own. It's the mother-child relationship that's important. The fact that I haven't physically given birth to them doesn't matter.'

Some women go on happily to adopt but still regret missing out on the experience of pregnancy and childbirth. 'I still feel I would like to have given birth to her myself. Our relationship is very good and I couldn't love her more if I had given birth to her myself, but I wish she had come out of my body.'

For other women, the key to their desire for motherhood lies in being pregnant and giving birth. 'The birth and the pregnancy, they are part of the reason why I wouldn't want to adopt. I think it's such a vital part of having a baby.'

Pregnancy and childbirth are given much publicity and attention today. You may not find it easy to forego such an emotionally powerful experience and give up being at the centre of so much attention. Going through childbirth is your passport to the community of mothers; you will have your own story to relate and you can compare notes with other women. Relating childbirth experiences is part of the currency of women.

Every time there is a new baby in the family, my female relatives all sit round and talk about their confinements. They all chip in with bits about how long their labours were, or how big their babies were, or whether the father got to the hospital in time to see the baby born.

If you adopt a child you cannot take part in the talk of childbirth; but remember, mothers' talk does not focus exclusively on childbirth; and when it is children, their pleasures and their problems, that are discussed, you are a mother just like the rest.

A child as a product of your relationship

Children are often talked about as being the product of your relationship. In this context, the joining of the egg and the sperm in some way reflects your closeness and is evidence of your joint commitment to a shared project. Adopting a child means that neither of you is involved physically or genetically in the start of the child's life. Some women express regret that an adopted child is not related biologically to them and their partner; expressions used commonly such as 'he's just like his dad, same hair and fiery temper' or 'her sister was just as difficult at that age' illustrate the generally held belief that certain physical and behavioural characteristics can be inherited. Certainly there is some evidence that some physical characteristics are genetically based, so that parents who are tall or fair-haired are more likely than other parents to have a child who is tall or fair-haired. But a quick glance at any family shows that there is a large element of luck as to which characteristics are indeed found in the next generation. The principles of genetics are far too complex to allow accurate predictions and, more importantly, there is little reason to believe that parents find it more difficult to love those children who look different from them. When we move away from physical characteristics to behavioural characteristics such as temperament, or being good at sports or maths, then the evidence for genetic transmission becomes much more suspect; how a child is brought up may be much more important in deciding how it develops.

For some people, adopting a child is difficult to think about because it means giving up on their desire for a child that is in some way a product of their life together. But adoption is a joint venture, one which is a strong expression of your relationship with your partner. It may take time to reconcile yourself to not knowing about the child's parents and to cope with the worries about how the child might develop. But all parents worry about how their children might turn out; and studies of adopted children suggest that they grow up to be normal, bright and emotionally stable children.[6]

Relating to the child

You may be concerned about the child's emotional and physical state, about the impact of adoption on it and you may be worried in case you find difficulties in developing a stable relationship between the two of you. So much importance is placed on making a good relationship early in the child's life and even with an early adoption you may worry that the first weeks or months before the child is in your care may have a damaging effect.

> I'm very lucky, I bonded with her immediately. It was incredible. I don't know what it feels like to bond with a child you've given birth to, but I don't suppose it's any different. It was so intense, perhaps too intense. She is very close to me. And yet they say that bonding can only happen after birth. But you see, she had very little chance to bond with anyone as far as I can tell, because she had been in an incubator for two months and then she had been with a foster mother who had three other children to look after. So I imagine she was ready to bond with anyone.

If you consider adopting an older child, then how do the experiences of its earlier years affect it? What happened in the child's early life? Had it been well cared for? Had it been loved or stimulated? Would you be able to establish a strong and loving relationship with it? An older child has experiences and memories you cannot share and you may worry that these may make it difficult for the child to accept its new family. These are serious worries and ones for which there are no clear answers. The lengthy legal procedures before a formal adoption takes place allows you plenty of time to decide whether a satisfactory relationship between you is possible. But one of the sadder aspects of adopting an older child is that your relationship will be shorter, soon he or she will be independent and perhaps leave your home.

At the time we were prepared to adopt an older child. We wouldn't have known what we missed. I still think it's a good thing to do if there is no alternative. You still have a lot of the child's life left to share. But there is no doubt about it, you miss out on a lot.

You may feel that if you are serious about wanting a child then you should be able to welcome a child of any age, of mixed race, or a disabled child – what are known to adoption agencies as 'hard to place' children.

I'm not sure about adopting handicapped children. It seems to me that if you're a novice parent, to pick up a difficult child, a child who's handicapped or been in care for many years, it would be very hard. If it were a second or third child, you'd know what to expect and you could take it on. But if you started off that way, well, I think you could be overloading your circuits.

These are real issues and ones which you need to think about. But many of the issues involved would crop up if you were pregnant with your own child. Like having children, adoption is a step into the unknown. No parents can be given complete assurance that they will get on with their children, nor that the child will like them. Perhaps as an infertile person, you feel more vulnerable and your anxieties about your parenting skills come more readily to mind. These anxieties quickly recede in the hurly-burly of rearing a child.

Other people's reactions
Your ideas about adoption also depend upon the reactions of those around you. The reactions of your partner are especially important. Some agencies consider single people as adoptive parents but most require or at least prefer adoptive parents to be married couples.

If you are hoping to adopt as a couple the active participation of both you and your partner is required at all stages. This may contrast starkly with your infertility investigations which may have asked very little of your partner. Adoption procedures take a long time and demand that you both talk about yourselves and your ideas about children. Your partner may be unwilling to think about adoption or he may take much longer than you do to be able to consider it as a possibility. He may not feel the grief of childlessness so acutely, he may not be as willing as you are to persist in the search for a child, or may feel unequal to parenting an adopted child. Should his objections persist, you may find reluctantly that you are forced to progress with the adoption at his pace, or to give up your ideas of adopting altogether.

On the other hand, you may find the joint involvement in the decision to try to adopt very positive. Unlike the infertility investigations,

129

adoption may provide a solution to your childlessness in which you are both engaged, and which reinforces the bonds between you.

Adoption means making a public statement about your infertility: in the past, you may have found it very difficult to talk about it and pretended to be indifferent about having children. Once you adopt, everyone knows that you did really want children but that you could not have your own.

While you and your partner may feel positive about adoption you may still worry that your family might feel differently as their ideas developed at a different time and in a different climate to your own. An adopted child not only makes you into a parent, but your own parents into grandparents, and so on.

> We were concerned about how my parents would take to an adopted child. I've always considered that they favoured my sister who has three children. I did wonder whether they would take to our child. But they have been really excited with him, and made such a fuss of him. They have accepted him as their own grandchild.

Going through adoption procedures

Having decided that you want to go ahead with adoption, your next step is to get your application accepted by an adoption agency. The British Agencies for Adoption and Fostering, formerly the Association of British Adoption and Fostering Agencies, publish a booklet containing a list of all the agencies together with their criteria. Details of this are given in the Appendix. You can apply directly to local authority social services departments, many of which advertise 'hard to place' children in newspapers and magazines. Many agencies periodically close their books when they have sufficient people undergoing assessment. So if you receive a reply informing you that lists are closed, you can try again to see if the lists have reopened. The agencies themselves do not inform you when this happens, nor is there much co-operation between them, so you need to be prepared to spend time and energy finding an agency willing to consider you.

> We got the book and wrote to twenty-six agencies. Half of them said no and the rest sent us a short form to fill in which I suppose they filed in the waste-paper basket. About half a dozen invited us to meetings where they tell you that there are no babies available for adoption. After that we gave up. We began to consider the possibility of being a childless couple and adjusted ourselves to that.

If an adoption agency is ready to consider you, then both you and your partner are assessed. Assessment involves a whole series of procedures, including a medical examination as well as a series of interviews with yourself and your partner by a social worker. The sort of questions you might be asked are: Why do you want a baby? Which kind of child are you prepared to adopt? Why did you marry your partner? You will also be asked about your parents and their relationship and how they brought you up, and about your relationship with your partner including your sexual relationship.

> Some of the questions they ask are impossible to answer like, why do you want a baby? What can you say? Anything you say sounds dreadful. I can't think of any logical reason that would sound okay to a social worker. If you walk round any maternity ward and ask all the mothers there why they wanted a baby, they wouldn't be able to give you a good answer. I found that a very difficult question.

You may find questions about your sex life very painful coming so soon after your infertility investigations. Few of us can have remained unaffected by repeated 'sex to order' for post-coital tests or for conception. Social workers should understand that sexual relations may for some be an indication of a harmonious relationship, but the investigations may have had a detrimental effect on the quality of the sex life of infertile women and men and it may take some time to recover.

You are also required to provide the social worker with details of your financial status.

> They wanted to know the value of the house, the size of the mortgage, his income, my income, you name any financial detail, and they wanted to know it. I could see them doing sums in their head. We were very astounded that they were far more concerned with our material wealth than with our emotional security.

The aim of the investigation is to decide whether you might make the kind of parent the agency feels is right for the child it is placing. Many people, both parents and non-parents, would fail to match up to the strict criteria used. Being investigated in this way can be painful for infertile people. Having to talk about yourself probably stirs up again all your pain and your feelings of how unfair it all is. If you were able to have your own children, then your life, your relationship and your motives would not be under this kind of scrutiny. But these are not feelings you are free to express; you feel you must sound positive and committed and as selfless as you can. You are asked to talk about yourself to someone who is in a position of power. It is this same social worker whose report influences strongly whether you are accepted as an adoptive parent. It is no wonder that so many women found the interviews uncomfortable.

> We tried to act as normally as possible, but it was very difficult. It's very trying, especially the first interview because you feel as though you are on trial. They come and ask you all sorts of things but they don't give you a chance to ask them any questions.

With the increasing number of older children, children in care and 'hard to place' children coming forward for adoption, some agencies are developing assessment procedures which are more child-oriented. Instead of being looked at as a potential parent in a vacuum, you are considered as the potential parent of a particular child or number of children which the agency hopes to place. From the start, you receive information about that child or children and if the child is old enough, he or she may also have a part in the assessment. You may find such agencies easier to deal with.

> They consider absolutely anybody; you just need to want a child. Their approach is completely different from other adoption agencies. You go through their literature until you see a child you would like to know more about. Then you and a social worker go into both your own and the child's situation. Do you realise what you may be letting yourself in for? Will you be able to cope? Then when you have considered it all carefully, with their help, if you still feel that this is a child you'd like to adopt, you are introduced to the child. Then you explore the situation with the child and if at the end of all that you still feel it's the right thing for you, then you can go ahead. Their attitude was so refreshing, it made such a change from the usual approach.

We give the addresses of agencies using this approach to adoption in the Appendix.

Adopting an older or disabled child is a big undertaking, so many agencies hold meetings for would-be adopters where people who have adopted such children talk about the problems and the pleasures they experience. These are group sessions so you also have an opportunity to talk to other people who, like you, are thinking about adoption.

Once you are accepted for adoption
Once you are accepted for adoption with the more traditional agencies, you wait for a child; this may take weeks, months or even years, depending on the availability of children and the sort of children you are prepared to accept. This can be a very fraught experience; your hopes may be raised only to be dashed.

> We were eventually offered a baby boy. We rushed out and bought all the nappies and put them into soak. Then we got a letter saying we couldn't have him after all, his mother had changed her mind. So we hung the nappies out to dry and put them away. Next, they rang up to say that a baby had just been born but that she was very premature. They said, come down and see her and that we could have her the next day. So we packed all the stuff into the car and down we went. We got to the foster mother who was in tears. The mother had been there the night before and had been hysterical. She said she couldn't part with the baby. So we went away empty handed again. We thought we'd go to my mums and get away from it all. While we were there, the social worker rang and said it was on again, could we come and collect her. Just as we were leaving,

the phone went and she said, no, we couldn't have her. So we went home and eventually she rang up and said it's on again, we could have the baby. So we finally got her.

If the adoption assessment has been centred around a particular child, then the process is a lot quicker. Often, such children are gradually introduced into your home, staying for weekends and then weeks before finally coming to live with you permanently.

Now is the time when you feel more confident about telling people about the adoption. It can feel exciting to be able to give good news after all the bad times you have been through.

In the United Kingdom, an adopted child is not legally your own until after the court hearing. Till then, the biological mother is allowed to change her mind and so there is always a possibility that you may lose the child. This is a tense time for adoptive parents, trying to get to know and to love their child, but anxious lest the biological mother changes her mind or the courts decide that they are unfit parents.

We never called her by name until we had gone to court. It was very nerve-wracking waiting till then. The mother's parents were very opposed to us having her because she is black and they didn't want her to go to a white family. But there aren't many black families coming forward to adopt. Anyway, they managed to convince them although they weren't very happy about it. Right up to the last minute, I was sure something would go wrong.

OTHER KINDS OF CHILDCARE

For one reason or another, you may rule out adoption and instead you may wish to consider other kinds of child-care such as fostering or involving yourself in the care of other women's children.

Fostering

Fostering agencies are always looking for new foster homes and it is comparatively easy to become a foster parent. But fostering may satisfy only a few of the needs of the involuntary childless. Like adoption, fostering gives you a child, but unlike adoption it is not yours permanently. Knowing that the child will or may leave you limits the involvement you are able to have in his or her life. You may find it difficult to enter fully into a commitment which will probably be short-lived – in which case fostering for you may be an unsatisfactory route to parenthood.

Fostering means considerable involvement with the social services. Although adoptive parents are subject to similar surveillance prior to adoption, once the child is theirs legally, contact with the social services ends, whereas with fostering links with social services are always maintained.

If you already have a child, then adding to your family through fostering may seem more acceptable. You have proved yourself by bringing up your own child successfully so you may feel more competent and secure as a mother and less threatened by the temporary nature of the fostering relationship.

Caring for other women's children

Getting involved with other women's children can be a response to childlessness, but it is one which infertile women often feel is hard to carry through.[7] Without children of your own, your experience of them may be minimal; they may appear to inhabit a distant world, one which you feel is not easy to approach. Often, it is assumed that childless people do not like children and are embarrassed by them.

> There's this notion that if you don't actually have kids, you don't want to be pestered by them, you don't like them. My friends never ask me to babysit for them. I'm convinced that they think I won't know what to do.

Of course, this may in fact be the case. We live in a society which is fairly strictly segregated into groups with similar social situations, and so unless we are parents ourselves, we may have little opportunity to learn the ways of being with children. And if it is assumed that you are hostile to or awkward with children, then you are rarely invited to join in children's activities. The less able you feel around children, the less contact you have, leaving you with little opportunity to develop any confidence around them. Then again, infertility can make you feel very self-conscious with children and afraid that you may be over-reacting or behaving strangely. 'When I see babies in prams, and I don't know many, just the odd friend who's got one, then I always feel terribly emotional. I worry that perhaps I'm being too nice about them, too enthusiastic.'

You may not welcome contact with children, finding them a painful reminder of your grief. Friends may try to draw you in, to share their experience, perhaps wanting you to share their pleasures. You may feel that you are being offered a slice of the cake when what you really want is the whole of it. 'When a friend of mine had her baby, she wanted me to be involved with it. But I thought it wouldn't work. Whatever she did would be wrong; the point is it's her baby, she's got one and I haven't.' On such occasions you need to express your feelings, to be able to thank a friend for her offer but to explain that it is not really helpful, at this moment anyway.

Women without children are often urged to become involved in childcare, either to babysit so that mothers can have time for themselves, or to take the child/children on a more regular basis as an attempt to set up an alternative to the nuclear family. Easing the load of mothers by giving them space and time to themselves is an important thing to do, and it may provide voluntarily childless women with an alternative between the very child-centred world of mothers and an otherwise childless existence. But it should be recognised that for the infertile woman, such an involvement may involve pain.

Shared childcare, although very different from having your own child, may provide you with some of the satisfactions of being around children.

Given the way that we work and live, however, it may take much sensitivity and negotiation to ensure that both you and the mother feel positively about any arrangement you come to. If you babysit, you may see very little of the child who is in bed asleep. Helping mothers out may provide only a very minimal involvement with the children being cared for, and may give you a very inadequate reflection of the joys as well as the pressures and pains of parenthood. Becoming more heavily involved in shared childcare is not always easy to set up; it is not considered normal for childless women to really want to become so involved in the care of another woman's child. Childless women are more likely to be employed and so are not readily available to care for children during working hours. However close your relationship, intimate day-to-day contact with children who do not live with us can be difficult because we often live too far away from each other, transport may be inadequate and houses are rarely designed to cope with large households. All too often, childless women slip into the role of visitor providing special treats or taking the child out, leaving the mother with the regular care and responsibility. Mothers for their part may be reluctant to set up childcare arrangements which are satisfying to childless women. They may well feel that other women can freely move in and out of their and their children's lives and that their commitment may not be as deep or as long-term as their own. Consequently, feeling that they have got sole responsibility, mothers change their childcare arrangements or even move away without recognising that others may experience a sense of loss. By necessity, most mothers have become so accustomed to taking total responsibility for their child that they hold on to this even when they do not mean to do so and when they claim to behave differently.

> All of my friends expressed the need not to be possessive of their children before they had them, and now they're all intensely possessive. I find this quite unnerving. Even though they've said my child is your child, I'm allowed very little. Fair enough, I'm not changing their nappies or getting up in the middle of the night. I don't really begrudge them, it's just that I'm really shocked to discover that all those things they said actually meant nothing.

Care, control, responsibility and love tend to come together in a package. For childcare to be satisfying to both parent and non-parent alike, a share of each of these elements is necessary.

> I think that if I'm cooking the tea, it ought to be up to me to decide whether or not the kids can have a sandwich beforehand, but when they go and ask their mother, she'll say yes or no regardless of me making the tea.

But even if she relinquishes some of her control on a day-to-day basis, in the long term, it is the mother who makes the decisions. In *Daughters of Jerusalem*, Liz discusses this problem with her friend Nancy.[8]

> 'But the responsibility is half the point. I have a pretty good

relationship with your kids, and some kind of pleasant friendship with Paula's boys too, but I'm dependent on your kindness.'

'No, no. I on yours.'

'Look, I take them to the park some Saturdays or Harri swimming once a fortnight if she's lucky. It's nice, but it hardly helps you with the whole shitty reality of the dirty nappies. And if you and I fell out, or even if you wanted to move house, or job, then the last thing you would think of – quite reasonably – would be my relationship with your kids, my loss of their friendship . . . You feel a responsibility for those kids and sometimes resent that you can't share it. I feel friendship and resent that it doesn't earn me responsibility. But I don't have any control. Even if we lived in an ideal commune, I might have more daily contact and stuff, but it would still be because you choose it so, and you could unchoose it any day you wanted.'

Involvement with other people's children can bring certain kinds of pleasures and can help to relieve the mother's load. It is a less extensive experience than rearing your own child and it does not bring with it the responsibility and control which is the power as well as the burden of motherhood. For some women, it may seem like a pleasant alternative to rearing their own child, whereas for others, it may seem like a pale reflection.

10

COPING WITH INFERTILITY

Infertility is a life crisis. How you cope with this crisis depends on a number of factors: the success of the strategies you have developed to deal with other crises in your life and whether these prove suitable to the crisis of involuntary childlessness; your reasons for wanting a child in the first place and the impact your inability to bear one has on other areas of your life; if a cause for your infertility is found, you have to cope with the problem of 'blame' and decide to what lengths you are prepared to go to try to have a child; and finally, whether you do or do not get pregnant and deliver a baby successfully.

Infertility is an experience which fluctuates in intensity and direction, so that at each stage you may have different needs and experience different emotions. As you progress through it, your ideas and emotions shift in order to accommodate your experience. At one point, infertility shapes you and at the next, you alter its direction. The ways in which you cope change according to the stage you are at. At the beginning of your investigations, a particular strategy may prove helpful in coping which later on you find useless. In chapter 4, we looked at going through infertility investigations and treatment. In this chapter, we concentrate on the ways in which you cope with your childlessness, examining some of the decisions you may have to make, and how those of us who remain childless can try to reconcile ourselves to it.

Two out of every three women who seek help eventually conceive and have children, one way or another. These women have to adjust to the alteration in their life plans. They have to accommodate the fact that it was not easy for them to conceive, that they had to go through investigations and that they had children later than they anticipated. Their image of themselves as fertile women is challenged. For these women, infertility is a sad phase in their lives. The pregnancy of infertile women who ultimately conceive is discussed in chapter 9. Hopefully, this negative experience makes them more able to recognise and respond to the needs of other women.

But one out of every three women who goes for help does not get pregnant. Some go on to adopt, but as adoption becomes less and less feasible as an alternative, more women have to reconcile themselves to their childlessness. This is a sad thing to have to do; the pain may fade but it is something which may never disappear completely.

In this chapter we try to look at infertility positively, to see what we have learnt from this experience about ourselves and our needs. We hope thereby to expand our understanding of women's experience generally, and base it more in reality.

TAKING CONTROL

Infertility is often experienced as losing control over life plans as well as over bodily functioning. You may feel as though you are living in limbo, waiting to find out if you are ever to have a child. The reason for your infertility may be established early in your investigations – for example, your partner is infertile or your Fallopian tubes are blocked. In these cases, your options are relatively clear and you have concrete issues to deal with. We are not trying to imply that these issues are easy to confront, nevertheless they do provide you with an explanation which enables you to make sense of what is happening. For other women, infertility investigations may fail to establish a cause: the results of the test are never sufficiently conclusive to pinpoint where the problem lies; you and your partner may not score very highly on any of the tests, but neither is your score low enough to pinpoint where the problem lies. You can respond to this uncertainty in one of two ways: either you accept that you and your partner are in some way to 'blame' for not responding to scientific medicine, or you realise that, to date, little is known about infertility and that more research is needed so that cases such as yours can be correctly diagnosed and treated. Should no clear reason for your infertility emerge, you have to decide how much longer you want to continue with the investigations. You may feel that it is not very productive to go on investing more time and energy in going for more tests or treatment. The alternative to this is to confront your childlessness.

Taking control means ceasing to be a victim of your infertility, moving on and looking at other aspects of your life. 'If only there was some way of returning to the person I was and the life I led before I started trying to get pregnant.'

Unfortunately, it is not possible to return to the point at which you started, to un-think your desire to have a child. Once you made that decision, only a great effort in self-denial would enable you to forget it. Your only real choice is to go forward. Taking control may mean different things at different stages in your infertility; so that in the beginning, you decide to undergo investigation which may lead you to a particular course of treatment. Later, you may decide to approach adoption agencies or to develop other areas of your life to fill the space you made for a child.

Trying to find out why you are infertile, or persisting with a particular form of treatment, are important goals and may colour much of your thoughts at the early stages of your infertility. But once you have found out what is wrong or have decided that there is no help available or that your treatment is not working, then staying with 'Why am I infertile?' may only hamper your coping and resolution.

So taking control can mean a wide variety of things at different points in your infertility history. It can mean going for treatment or adoption, but it can also mean deciding to call a halt to the proceedings and moving on to other things.

Time plays an important part throughout, but its role differs from woman to woman. Time creates its own dynamic but it is also something which you can use yourself to shape the direction of your infertility. You cannot determine how long it takes to discover the cause of your infertility, nor how long a treatment needs to work. You cannot determine the pace at which your adoption agency works, nor how quickly your application is processed and how soon after that you are given a child. But what you *can* do is to some extent pace each new chapter in your infertility story according to your ability to cope with every new intrusion. Sometimes it feels as though your infertility has a life of its own, one which may put you under pressure to proceed at a faster rate than you feel able to deal with. Each new move may take some time to come to terms with, to allow you to adjust your ideas and to decide what you feel capable of taking on. It is important to remember that it is *your* body and *your* life, and you do not have to proceed with any investigations until you are ready, if at all.

Time works for and against you. The longer you leave your decision to have a child, to proceed with a particular form of treatment or to apply for adoption, the less chance you have of success. All childless women in their thirties feel under pressure to make decisions quickly before their fertility declines, or before they are considered too old to be adoptive parents. Infertile women are constantly reminded that time is running out; in particular women with endometriosis are advised to get pregnant as quickly as possible to cure their condition or before the disease spreads so far that a hysterectomy is unavoidable. These are realistic constraints on your ability to pace your progress through the various procedures. But time does heal many things, including the pain of your infertility. The pain lessens over time and in a matter of years your friends will be less engrossed in their own childbearing and rearing; soon like you, they are leading child-free existences. At menopause, all women lose their fertility and you will no longer be alone and different with your infertility.

It is often said that for a successful resolution of any life crisis, it is important to grieve and to be allowed to grieve.[1] Grief and mourning proceed through different stages: shock and disbelief, followed by denial and then anger and depression, and then resolution. You may or may not experience each of these stages. People work through the stages at different rates. In months or years to come, you may be surprised to find that your infertility re-emerges and that one stage of grieving still needs to be worked through.

> On my fortieth birthday, I felt really sad. I realised that I would never have a child. I'd always thought that when I was forty, I'd have young kids, so although it was years since I'd thought about it, I felt very sad.

For some, the process of grief may be short-lived, whereas for others it may take longer to complete.[ ] The grief of the infertile woman, unlike other losses and disappointments has no focus, no clear loss to mourn. There are ways you can help yourself to grieve: you can concentrate on it; you can throw yourself into it; you can seek help from a counsellor or a psychotherapist sympathetic towards women; or you may feel that contact with other infertile women may be helpful, allowing you to share your experiences and support each other. One woman describes her attempts to help herself.

> Somehow, I've got to cope. I think you have to look for things that are going to help you to cope and help you to get over it. I think one of these things is that I have got to do is to forgive myself for feeling down and for feeling sad. If I'm going to live a reasonable life, one with some richness, then I've got to find the things that are satisfying, and concentrate on them whilst I recover.

Two organisations have been set up to help infertile men and women, the National Association for the Childless (NAC) and Child. They both try to help in practical ways and to provide emotional support, both are non-profit-making and their membership is open to infertile individuals and couples, to those who go on to have children, and to professionals involved in infertility and adoption. NAC produces a number of helpful pamphlets on the causes and treatments of infertility and both publish articles in their quarterly newsletters on its medical and social aspects. They are important organisations fighting for the rights of infertile people, pushing for improvements in infertility research and infertility services. Child also operates a 24-hour telephone answering service. Both organisations concentrate on the needs of heterosexual couples and neither challenge the ways in which the organisation of our society and especially the nuclear family is responsible for much of the anguish of the infertile.

A very different organisation is the British Association of Non-Parents (BON). This organisation offers the infertile a way of looking at their infertility in the context of the social pressures to have children. One of its aims is to break the assumption that a fulfilled and satisfying life can only be a life which includes your own children. This assumption is clearly one which creates problems for infertile as well as childless-by-choice people. If you think your future lies in working on the positive aspects of a childless life, then BON may be helpful. (Addresses of these three organisations are given in the Appendix.)

CREATING A NEW IDENTITY

Coping with your infertility means coming to accept yourself as a childless person. You are a woman without children, no more, no less. In our society childrearing is one of the main areas in which women are expected to devote their energies; but you cannot apply yourself to this endeavour and it does not help that other women can. For those of us whose earlier years were focused on surviving as women in a man's world, it can be very confusing not to be able to bear children like other women. In the past we have devalued the role of motherhood, believing it to be oppressive and feeling that most women had little choice about becoming mothers, but we were always certain that if we wanted to have children we would be able to do so.

By whatever route you came to the decision to have a child, your self-esteem has been battered by your infertility. Coping and coming to terms with it means coming to see yourself as all right again. Like other women without children, like women who have chosen not to have them, or like older women whose children have grown up, you are a person who can be loved, liked and lusted after. Children in themselves do not make you any more or less likeable, womanly, able to relate to other people or productive in other areas of your life. In fact the contrary may well be true. Women with children have less time and energy to give to other people and to develop other interests outside their families.

Creating a new identity without children is an important part of asserting control over your infertility. This involves trying to think beyond children and deciding what you want for yourself.

> I've always worked but now I'd like to spend more time at home. We're hoping to move to a bigger house. I think I'll become a seaside landlady. I'd like to spend time on myself. It's time to think what I want outside of being pregnant. It's the first positive move I've made. If we're going to move away and buy the house, then I've got to think about what I want from life from now on, that it's not going to include children. I've been obsessed with children since I was eighteen. Now I'm thirty-two. I've spent so much of my life worrying about them. I've got to accept that that's the way it is and channel my energies into something else.

It involves giving up your desires for a child while not regretting the time you have spent in your quest.

> I feel that I mustn't regret too much the time I've wasted. I mustn't say why did I waste two years? I've got to start again, move into a new chapter. I've been drifting for too long hoping something would happen.

Creating a new identity does not mean abandoning your reasons for wanting a child. Just as those reasons shaped your infertility experience, so they affect the form that your resolution takes. Your new identity can accommodate some of the motives that you had for wanting a child. You need to be able to acknowledge and accept those ideas so you can build upon them, and take their essence into account. It is not a question of giving up ideas which seemed important, or of denying the power they had for you, but of looking for new ways of working on those ideas. Winifred Holtby in The Crowded Street talks in a similar way about what influenced Muriel's decision not to marry. 'She let me see, not that the thing that I had sought was not worth seeking, but simply that there were other things in life.'[2]

How can you incorporate your motives for wanting a child into your resolution of your childlessness? We look at some of the strategies available to you.

> I try to think about what I was like eighteen months ago before I

wanted a child. What used to make me happy? What did I look forward to? What did I want to do with my life? But I could never go back to that stage and pretend that a baby had never entered into the scheme of things. We used to lead a very full life, enjoying holidays and parties.

What you do and what activities you take up depend on the opportunities open to you. If you have a career you might find considerable support from it, offering you an identity outside motherhood, and reminding you constantly that it is possible to lead a satisfying and successful life without children. 'The fact that I have a job and a career is very important to me. I would give it all up for a baby, but knowing it is there has helped me enormously.'

Rather than changing your whole life, coping with your infertility may involve only readjusting your priorities, with greater effort going into your work. If you do not have a job, or are working in one which you do not enjoy but which you have kept, believing that you would soon be a mother, then the situation may be harder for you. It would be naive of us to suggest that you find an interesting career when the opportunities may not be available. But your responsibilities are fewer without children. In many ways you can afford to put yourself first, to look for a new job or to take a course, to look for something that you find interesting and to use your talents. Work and home are not the only two sources of satisfaction, there is a world of possibilities in between. 'I was quite prepared to do all kinds of things, to move house, to look for promotion in my job, to go back to college, to go into something entirely different, anything that would take me out of the rut I'd got in to.'

Being infertile may have given you plenty of opportunity to think about children and why you want them, and so you have gained some greater understanding of your needs and what having a child means to you. It allows you to focus and to work on the aspects of having children which are important to you.

One of the attractions of having children is that it is supposed to be a long-term relationship. Friends, lovers and fellow workers may all move on, but blood ties are thought of as permanent ties, even though they may be pretty deadening and claustrophobic at times. The desire for a child may come out of your need for stability and permanence. But a child is of course no guarantee; many women lead lives which are very separate from their parents. Any difficulties in the relationship with your parents may spur you on; you had imagined you would provide your children with the good and loving relationships that you did not have with your parents. Not having children has robbed you of an opportunity to show what a good parent you would be and what good children you would have. But it has not robbed you of all warm relationships; the self-insight you have gained into your own needs, the need to care and be cared for can be used in other, more equal relationships with adults.[3]

There are many pressures on women to have children in a society which sees the norm in terms of heterosexual couples with children. We have written this book having in mind all women who want children but are unable to bear them. We believe the plight of the single woman, the lesbian and the wife who finds herself infertile is basically similar, although each woman experiences it differently. Not having children makes you different whether it is through choice or because you are infertile – and some women find this very uncomfortable, especially if you feel happiest doing what everyone else does and not standing out in a crowd. Sadly there are still a limited number of acceptable roles for women in our society. Finding a comfortable and not too exposed niche may be a major aspect of your coping with infertility.

Mothers and non-mothers often seem to inhabit different worlds. Infertile women often long to join the world of mothers but feel that because they lack the credentials of having a child they would be viewed with suspicion. Mothers may envy the childless woman her freedom and perhaps her relative affluence.

Coping with your infertility can mean distancing yourself from the world of mothers and their children, removing yourself to a safe position and giving up any serious intentions of being involved with children. Another way of coping is to try and set up a third camp: being a woman without children of her own but still involved with children. This is a role which single and widowed women adopted in the past, taking children on outings or involving themselves in childcare on a more regular basis. But this is a role which needs working on: women without children often fear that they do not know what to do, that children will not like them, or that they will over-compensate and look foolish. And mothers may find it difficult to understand that another woman wants to look after her children, or she may feel threatened that another woman might be more skilful at looking after her children. To become involved in other women's children requires you to work on these issues.

Many women see children as a way in which they can be creative and can make their mark on the world. For them, coming to terms with their infertility means recognising that they have something to contribute in their own right. Too often women lack confidence in their ability to be able to do things themselves, or to be able to help others.

> I have more time. At work all the other women rush off to collect their children from school and leave me to tidy up and to deal with all the things which crop up after they've gone. So often I'm the first one there and the last one to leave. Sometimes that's very painful, that they have other more important things to rush off to. When I'm feeling better about it, I can see that that is what I can offer; that they can work better because I can clear up after them at the end of the day.

Having children or being with children gives you permission to do all the childish things that adults enjoy but are not supposed to indulge in such as playing games or watching children's television. Other activities are most acceptable when they focus on children, such as showing unconditional love, being affectionate and caring for another in a protective way. But all adults retain a childish side; it is a tragedy for mothers when caring for their children does not allow them sufficient opportunity to have their own needs met. One woman describes how powerful it can be to have those needs met.

> It can also be very pleasant to be in a situation where, for the first time, you don't immediately have the feeling you have to do something in return. Especially if, as a woman, you are accustomed to knowing that a caress on the back isn't meant to caress you, but to get something as quickly as possible. I have been present when a woman realising how much warmth she had been deprived of, asked her women's group to stroke and massage her for ten minutes. One person massaged her feet, another her neck, a third stroked her back. She cried for at least a quarter of an hour when she realised how she always gave – to her children, to her husband – and how little she received.[4]

So many mothers identify with their child, seeing the care and affection they lavish on them as a substitute for the lack of care the child in them receives. As a childless woman, it is important to discover new ways of caring and of being cared for, to have these needs met, to demand that the child in you is looked after as well as being aware of and looking after the child in others.

RELATIONSHIPS AND SEX

We have tried to show that the impact of infertility is twofold: directly through the effects on you and indirectly through the impact your infertility has on the people to whom you relate.

Infertility brings about changes in your relationships. Some may become too difficult and you drift away from one another; some take on new dimensions as the infertility creates new bonds between you, where it becomes possible for you to support one another. Some of these changes are sad ones, others are enriching. Whilst many of your involvements undergo change, it is probably the relationships with those closest to you which are most affected, and almost certainly, your sexual relations suffer. This is true whether you are a single woman, a lesbian or one of a heterosexual couple. Women's sexuality and sexual pleasure focus on the clitoris, but reproduction requires a concentration on the vagina and the hormonal changes of the menstrual cycle. In the pamphlet 'Self Insemination', a group of lesbians describe the lengths they went to in order to conceive. This makes the point clearly that for single women, lesbian or heterosexual, finding men to have sex with or paying for artificial insemination is both tedious and unpleasant. Taking months or years to become pregnant under such conditions is hardly an attractive prospect. For lesbians and their lovers, the sexual implications are no less important.

> I had to face how much the power the idea of the father had over me – my own sense that a biological relationship bestowed rights... I would be trying to construct a relationship without any

biological supports, based on my choices and the child's choices. The power of the father, the concept and the actuality, over Pauline, over the baby, over myself. I could not accept this, nor their sexual interaction — to be repeated how many times? — without being upset.[5]

For heterosexual women sex quickly loses many associations with pleasure, becoming instead an activity with a functional purpose.

We were pretty casual about it at first, when we started. But that's changed now. We've had sex three times a month for two and a half years expressly for a baby. That's ninety times in all. That's not fun, you've got to be serious to do that.

The pressure to have sex around the time of your ovulation and when the investigations demand imposes considerable pressures on a relationship. It may take many months, if not years for the pleasurable side of sex to return. To change the emphasis may require positive efforts on the part of each partner, such as trying to have sex on infertile days of the month. When one partner is to 'blame' and feels inadequate and guilty, this may be especially difficult.

I did feel I was failing him dreadfully and started to say things like, you should find a younger woman. I felt very strongly that it would affect our relationship in years to come, he might regret staying with me and wish he were with a younger woman.

In these situations it is true that there is always a solution for the fertile partner, to leave and look elsewhere for a parent of their child. If you are the fertile partner, it can be hard to handle your own feelings or fantasies about wishing you could find a way out or about leaving this man and finding someone else. If you are the infertile partner, then you may feel anxious that your partner will leave you. It would be falsely optimistic of us to say that all relationships survive infertility crises, but many do. Relationships based solely on a mutual desire for a child must be rare. It is important to recollect those aspects of each other that you found attractive before the investigations started and to try to recover old ways of relating to each other; and you need to find new ways too that are not centred around a child or anticipation of a child. It may seem hard to give up your dreams of a future which involves children and settle for one without. But ultimately, all parents have to find an identity beyond parenthood and it may be possible to gain strength by looking at women older than yourself to see how they cope with their loss, and how they adjust when their children no longer need their day-to-day care.

There are a number of ways of looking again at your relationships so you can work out new ways of relating which are not family-centred. You may try to find common interests to share, to bind you together. This closeness may give you strength. Or you could accept that without children you need not become a tight and cohesive unit, that you can each find new interests and enjoy other people without having to be continuously engaged in joint projects. Being less tied to the tasks of childrearing puts you in the position to relate to a wider range of people including older people whose children are independent, single people or people younger than yourself.

It would be wrong of us to underestimate the blow infertility has dealt to both you and your relationships. We know only too well that it takes a long time to recover, but it is a recovery that you must and will make. At times, you may feel inadequate and unable to handle new relationships, but being infertile does not stop you from being able to get close to other people and to have satisfying relationships.

HEALTH CARE AND CONTRACEPTION

One natural reaction to the intrusion of infertility investigations is to neglect health care or contraception. Women seeking contraceptive advice and mothers undergoing regular ante-natal or post-natal check-ups have other aspects of their health monitored. Many health checks are done as routine screening, for example, blood pressure, breast examination and cervical smears. These checks are still important to you and may require a special effort on your part to ensure that you receive them. GPs sometimes carry out routine screening, or you could find out if there is a Well Woman clinic in your area. It may take you some time before you are ready to face another physical examination, but it is important not to leave it too long.

> The thought of lying on a couch and having another hand inside my vagina is enough to give me hysterics. I've had so many internal examinations that I just can't face another.

If there is a clear reason for your infertility, then the issue of contraception may never arise as long as you remain in that relationship. If no clear reason is found, then you should not assume that you will never conceive. It is possible that you have restructured your life in such a way that children would be an intrusion so it may be wise for you to use some form of contraceptive, to avoid the problem of an unwanted pregnancy. Or you may decide not to use contraceptives because you prefer to keep alive the hope that one day you still may conceive. Or you may decide to use them, or even to become sterilised, because then at least you do not have to endure the agony of waiting, watching and wondering if you are pregnant each month. You may be able to accept your childlessness and move on to other things only with the knowledge that you cannot get pregnant.

POSTSCRIPT

In writing this book we have tried to make infertility more accessible and less alienating to women. We hope that women reading this book, both infertile women and others, can support each other and offer help.

I realise now that other women have been helped by my struggle; my friends will never face infertility unprepared. They will be forewarned and forearmed and experience it as a land for which they have already seen a map if only a rough and ready one. At least they will never feel that no one has stepped this way before.

NOTES

INTRODUCTION

1. Adrienne Rich, *Of Woman Born*, Virago, London, 1977. We found Adrienne Rich's discussion of motherhood both moving and stimulating. We are indebted to her for providing a framework for many of our ideas.
2. For a discussion of Margaret Sanger's life and work, see Margaret Sanger, *Motherhood in Bondage*, Vol 3, Margaret Sanger; An Autobiography. Dover, New York, 1971.
3. We spoke to about fifty women and tape-recorded twenty-two interviews. We contacted these women through advertisements, through a workshop we ran on infertility at a Women's Health Conference, but mainly through friends and friends of friends. For many of the women, speaking to us was the first time they felt able to talk at length about their infertility. The women were living in a variety of situations although most were in stable relationships with men. The quotes we have used come from our interviews.
4. Figures from the Office of Population and Census Surveys.

Chapter 2: THINKING ABOUT HAVING A CHILD

1. For figures on family size and composition see Lesley Rimmer, *Families in Focus: Marriage, Divorce and Family Patterns*, Study Commission on the Family, London, 1981.
2. See, for instance, Ann Oakley, *Becoming a Mother*, Martin Robertson, Oxford, 1979.
3. Robert Newill, *Childless Marriage*, Penguin, Harmondsworth, 1974, p.74.
4. Sara Maitland, *Daughters of Jerusalem*, Blond and Briggs, London, 1978, p. 236. This novel, written about a woman going through infertility investigations, is an excellent book and compulsive reading for any infertile woman.
5. Rich, *op. cit.*, p. 33.
6. Joan Busfield, 'Ideologies and Reproduction', in Martin P.M. Richards (ed), *The Integration of the Child into a Social World*, Cambridge University Press, London, 1974.
7. Oakley, *op. cit.*, p. 33.
8. David Rudkin, *Ashes*, Pluto, London, 1978, p. 20.
9. For a discussion of the risks involved in having a baby later in life, see ch. 9. See also Jane Price, *You're Not too Old to Have a Baby*, Penguin, Harmondsworth, 1979.
10. For a discussion of reproductive hazards see F.M. Sullivan and Sue Barlow, 'Congenital Malformations and other Reproductive Hazards', *Proceedings of the Royal Society London*, B, 205, 1979, pp. 91–110; *Woman's Report*, Volume 7, Number 1, 2–4 December 1978/January 1979;Wendy Chavkin, 'Occupational Hazards to Reproduction', *Feminist Studies*, 5,2, summer 1979, pp. 310–325.
11. See for instance, L.B. Frankle, *The Ambivalence of Abortion*, Penguin, Harmondsworth, 1980, pp. 78–81.

12. Busfield, *op. cit.*, p. 15.
13. *Listener*, 11 December 1980, p. 783–786. For an interesting discussion of women's creativity, see Paula Weideger in *Why Children?* (eds.) Stephanie Dowrick and Sibyl Grundberg, The Women's Press, London, 1980.
14. John and Elizabeth Newson, *Seven Years Old in the Home Environment*, Penguin, Harmondsworth, 1976. Ch. 12, 'Towards an understanding of the parental role', pp. 436–446.
15. Busfield, *op. cit.*, p. 18.
16. *ibid.* for a discussion of sex composition. Also, Nancy Williamson, *Sons or Daughters? A Cross Cultural Study of Parental Preferences*, Sage Library of Social Research, London, 1976.
17. The Women and Science Collective, *The Politics of Contraception*, London, 1977; Eric McGraw, 'Proposals for a National Policy on Population, *Population Concern*, 9, London, 1981; Adrienne Rich, *Of Woman Born*, Virago, London, 1977, page 73–76 and 102.

CHAPTER 3: THINKING YOU MIGHT BE INFERTILE

1. For accounts of infertility see: Buchi Emecheta, *The Joys of Motherhood*, Heinemann, London, 1979; Adrienne D. Kraft, J. Palombo, D. Mitchell, C. Dean, S. Meyers and A.W. Schmidt, 'The Psychological Dimensions of Infertility', *American Journal of Orthopsychiatry*, 50, 1980, pp. 618–628; Miriam Mazor, 'The Problem of Infertility', in M.T. Norman and C.C. Nadelson (eds), *The Woman Patient*, Volume 1: *Sexual and Reproductive Aspects of Women's Health Care*, London: Plenum, 1978 Barbara E. Menning, 'The Emotional Needs of Infertile Couples', *Fertility and Sterility*, 34, 313–319, 1980; Jo Pollentine, 'Facing Infertility', *Spare Rib*, 117, April 1982, pp. 50–53.
2. Helen Roberts, *Guardian*, 17 November, 1981.
3. Figures on Infertility are not easy to find. Clues about how long it takes to get pregnant come from a variety of sources: Gordon Bourne, *Pregnancy*, Pan, London, 1975; Ann Cartwright, *How Many Children*, Routledge, London, 1976 (In a sample of mothers, 19 per cent took more than a year to conceive.); Derek Llewelyn-Jones, *Fundamentals of Obstetrics and Gynaecology*, Volume 2, Faber, London, 1978, Ch. 10 states that 90 per cent of women not using a contraceptive conceive in twelve months.
4. Angela Phillips and Jill Rakusen, *Our Bodies Ourselves*, Penguin, Harmondsworth, 1978, p. 241 suggests in a discussion of contraceptive failure that 10 per cent of women who are sexually active and using no contraceptive are not pregnant after one year.
5. *ibid.* In most respects this is an excellent book, but even here, 97 pages (17 per cent of the book) are devoted to contraception and abortion, 15 pages to whether to have a child or not and 13½ pages to infertility and miscarriage. The discussion of infertility is separated by 143 pages from the discussion of choosing parenthood.
6. For a discussion of how long it took people to be referred for infertility investigations see David J. Owens and M.W. Read, 'The Provision, Use and Evaluation of Medical Services for the Subfertile: An Analysis Based on the Experiences of Involuntary Childless Couples', SRU Working Paper, Number 4, University of Cardiff, 1979.
7. Joan Busfield, 'Ideologies and Reproduction', in Martin P.M. Richards (ed), *The Integration of the Child into a Social World*, Cambridge University Press, London, 1974, page 28.
8. The medical textbooks on infertility tend to discuss causes only briefly, and to focus on the more esoteric causes. See for instance: Derek Llewelyn Jones *Fundamentals of Obstetrics and Gynaecology*, Volume 2, Faber, London, 1978;

John Stangel, *Fertility and Conception*, Paddington Press, London, 1979;R.J. Pepperell, Bryan Hudson and Carl Wood (eds), *The Infertile Couple*, Churchill Livingstone, New York, 1980; Leon Speroff, Robert H. Glass and Nathan G. Kase, *Clinical Gynaecologic Endocrinology and Infertility*, Williams and Williams, Baltimore, 1978; Elliot Phillip and Barry Carruthers (eds), *Infertility*, Heinemann Medical Books, London, 1981.

For a more critical discussion of the causes of infertility see Federation of Feminist Women's Health Centres, *How to Stay Out of the Gynaecologist's Office* Peace Press, California, 1982.

9. F.M. Sullivan and Sue Barlow, 'Congenital Malformations and other Reproductive Hazards, *Proceedings of the Royal Society London*, B, 205, 1979, page 91–110. Wendy Chavkin, 'Occupational Hazards to Reproduction', *Feminist Studies*, 5,2, summer 1979, pp. 310–325.

10. Buchi Emecheta, *The Joys of Motherhood*, Heinemann, London, 1979. page 12.

For a discussion of infertility in other cultures, see: Ronald L. Kleinman and Pramilla Senanayake (eds), *Handbook on Infertility*, International Planned Parenthood Federation, London, 1979; *People*, International Planned Parenthood Federation, Vol 5, No. 1, 1978.

11. Again, the figures are not easy to come by. These figures are an average of those given in a number of medical source books, including those referred to in this and subsequent chapters.

12. Federation of Feminist Women's Health Centres, *op. cit.*

13. G.L. Christie, 'The Psychological and Social Management of the Infertile Couple', in R.J. Pepperell, Bryan Hudson and Carl Wood (eds), *The Infertile Couple*, Churchill Livingstone, New York, 1980, p.238.

14. Sara Maitland, *Daughters of Jerusalem*, Blond and Briggs, London, 1978, page 65.

15. *ibid.*, pp. 178–179.

16. Irene Klepfisz in Stephanie Dowrick and Sibyl Grundberg (eds), *Why Children?*, The Women's Press, London, 1980, page 25.

CHAPTER 4: GOING THROUGH INFERTILITY INVESTIGATIONS

1. In an unquoted source *Our Bodies Ourselves* say 13 per cent of women conceive after a first visit to the doctor. Angela Phillips and Jill Rakusen, *Our Bodies Ourselves*, Penguin, Harmondsworth, 1978, p.493.

For a critique of the magic of the first appointment see Terrance S. Drake and Donald R. Tredway, 'Spontaneous Pregnancy during the Infertility Evaluation', *Fertility and Sterility*, 30, 1978, pp.36–38.

2. David J. Owens and Martin W. Read, 'The Provision, Use and Evaluation of Medical Services for the Subfertile', SRU Working Paper 4, University of Cardiff, 1979, p. 8 and 50 found that 'those couples who remained on the NHS fared as well generally as those couples who went privately ... it does seem that the private sector offered little advantage in terms of availability of tests for the wives ... there is no appreciable difference in the tests offered to men who saw a specialist privately than for those men who remained with the NHS ... There was some indication that private treatment was quicker than treatment on the NHS and that private doctors were the more sympathetic.'

3. Elliot Philipp, *Childlessness*, Arrow, London, 1975, p.30. This book lists the following medical practitioners available to help a childless couple: G.P., Gynaecologist (Medical), Gynaecologist (Surgeon), Andrologist, Urologist, Clinic Secretary, Clinic Sister, Clinic Social Worker, Histologist, Radiologist, Endocrinologist, Biochemist, Geneticist, Psychiatrist.

4. *ibid.*, p.29.

5. For a discussion on what should count as a criterion of success in the treatment of infertility see E. E. Wallach, 'Tubal Reconstructive Surgery', *Fertility and Sterility*, 34, 1980, pp.531–533.

6. For an outline of the doctor's view of the first appointment see Philipp, *op. cit.*, chapters 4 and 5; Andrew Stanway, *Why Us?*, Granada, St Albans, 1980, chapter 5.

7. G.L. Christie, 'The Psychological and Social Management of the Infertile Couple', in R.J. Pepperell, Bryan Hudson, Carl Wood (eds), *The Infertile Couple*, Churchill Livingstone, New York, 1980, page 239.

8. See, for instance, Stanway, *op. cit.*, p. 102.

9. See, for instance, the quick addition of psychological causes only after discussion of the medical causes is complete. For a discussion of psychological factors see Stanway, *op. cit.*, chapter 6; Phillip, *op. cit.*, chapter 12; Pepperell, Hudson, Wood (eds), *op. cit.*, chapter 11; L. Carenza and L. Zichella (eds), *Proceedings of Serono Symposia*, Vol 20A, Emotion and Reproduction, pp. 261–318; R. Newill, *NACK*, January 1981, number 20, pp. 16–17.

10. 'The available data do not permit any statement about linking personality factors as causal to female infertility. If this does indeed exist, its proof will come only when the rules of scientific experimentation are followed by gynaecologists, obstetricians and psychiatrists, just as they are by all scientists, in well-designed and controlled studies with meaningful numbers. These criteria have not been met by the presently available anecdotal case reports or even from the fragments of the psychoanalysis of one patient or from psychotherapy of several patients.' Herman C.B. Denber, 'Psychiatric Aspects of Infertility', *Journal of Reproductive Medicine*, 20, pp. 23–29.

And 'If your doctor, having tested you and your partner completely says your problem is psychological, react with healthy disbelief'... 'The most pressing psychological aspect of infertility is not as cause but rather as effect.' From Jill Turner and Wendy Savage, *The Good Health Guide for Women*, British edition, London, Hamlyn, 1981, p. 104.

11. 'Simply on statistical grounds, doctors alone cannot cope with the problem (sexual disorders)... Nor are they always the best equipped to cope, as the very nature of their training can inhibit the development of those qualities of personality most necessary for effectiveness as a sex therapist.' 'Doctors and Sexual Disorders', *Journal of the Royal Society of Medicine*, Volume 74, May 1981, pp. 390–391.

And 'Most doctors unfortunately are still ill prepared to deal with sexual problems. Until very recently, the discussion of sexual dysfunctions and their treatment was not part of a regular school curriculum and in many places it still isn't.' Albert Decker and Suzanne Loebl, *We Want to Have a Baby*, Penguin, Harmondsworth, 1980, p. 166.

12. See, for instance, Derek Llewelyn Jones, *Fundamentals of Obstetrics and Gynaecology*, Volume 2, Faber, London 1978 p.96; John Newton and Anthony Johnson, 'The Investigation of the Infertile Couple', *Hospital Update*, December 1977, pp. 689–703.

13. Owens and Read, *op.cit.*, p. 31, found that only 50 per cent of patients surveyed had a diagnosis within twelve months.

14. See the very strict separation of tests and treatments in some discussions, for example, John Stangel, *Fertility and Conception*, Paddington Press, London, 1979; Phillips and Rakusen, *op.cit.*, chapter 15.

15. Terence J. Johnson, *Professions and Power*, Macmillan, London, 1972; Eliot Friedson, *The Profession of Medicine*, Dodd Mead, New York, 1975; Ivan Illich, *Limits to Medicine*, Penguin, Harmondsworth, 1977; Vicente Navarro, *Medicine Under Capitalism*, Prodist, New York, 1976.

16. Evelyn Billings, *The Billings Method: Controlling Fertility without Drugs or*

Devices, Allen Lane, London, 1980; Margaret Nofziger, *Cooperative Methods of Natural Birth Control*, Book Publishing Company, third edition, 1979, Simmertown, Tennessee; Art Rosenblum, *The Natural Birth Control Book*, Aquarian Research Foundation, 1976.

CHAPTER 5: MALE INFERTILITY AND 'ARTIFICIAL INSEMINATION BY DONOR' (AID)

1. David J. Owens and Martin W. Read, *The Provision, Use and Evaluation of Medical Services for the Subfertile*, SRU Working Paper 4. University of Cardiff, October 1979, pp. 27 and 31, found that men had semen tests and very little else, and that the length of their investigations was shorter than women's.
 For the only account of men's experience of infertility investigations see, David J. Owens, 'The Desire to Father: Reproductive Ideologies and Involuntarily Childless Men' in Lorna McKee and Margaret O'Brien (eds), *The Father Figure*, Tavistock, London, 1982.
2. Lawrence Dubin and Richard Amelar, *Fertility and Sterility*, 34, 1980, pp. 74–75, argue for a more scientific approach to male infertility.
3. Andrew Stanway, *Why Us?*, Granada, St Albans, 1980, p.45, says about emotional or stress factors in male infertility that 'while they are unlikely to play much of a part in a man (except if the condition make him unable to obtain or maintain an erection) they certainly play a very important role in women'.
4. Bryan Hudson, H.W.G. Baker, D.M. de Kretser, 'The Abnormal Semen Sample', in R.J. Pepperell, Bryan Hudson, Carl Wood, (eds) *The Infertile Couple*, Churchill Livingstone, New York, 1980, p.106.
5. Jan Friberg and Carl Gemzell, 'Sperm Freezing and Donor Insemination', *International Journal of Fertility*, 22, 1977, pp. 148–154.
6. For two accounts of running AID clinics see R.S. Ledward, L. Crawford, E.M. Symonds, 'Social Factors in Patients for Artificial Insemination by Donor (AID)', *Journal of Biosocial Science*, 11, 1979, pp. 473–479; Bernard Sandler, 'Adoption and Artificial Insemination by Donor (AID)' in Stephen Wolkind (ed), *Medical Aspects of Adoption and Foster Care*, S.I.M.P. London, 1979.
7. The Feminist Self Insemination Group, *Self Insemination*, London, 1980.
8. R. Snowden, G.D. Mitchell, *The Artificial Family*, George Allen and Unwin, London, 1981.

CHAPTER 6: INFERTILITY IN WOMEN: PROBLEMS IN CONCEIVING

1. See chapter 4, note 16.
2. J.P. Royston, R.M. Abrams, Mary P. Higgins and Anna M. Flynn, 'The Adjustment of Basal Body Temperature to Allow for Time of Waking', *British Journal of Obstetrics and Gynaecology*, 87, 1980, pp. 1123–1127.
3. For a good discussion of the techniques of detecting ovulation, see J.B. Brown, R.J. Pepperell, J.H. Evans, 'Disorders of Ovulation', in R.J. Pepperell, Bryan Hudson, Carl Wood, (eds), *The Infertile Couple*, Churchill Livingstone, New York, 1980, chapter 2. Kamran S. Moghissi, 'Prediction and Detection of Ovulation', *Fertility and Sterility*, 34, 1980, pp. 89–98. Joan E. Bauman, 'Basal Body Temperature: Unreliable Method of Ovulation Detection', *Fertility and Sterility*, 36, 1981, pp. 729–733.
4. Anna Wileman in Stephanie Dowrick and Sibyl Grundberg (eds) *Why Children?*, The Women's Press, London, 1980, pp. 213–228.
5. Doctors have very contradictory things to say about the discomfort involved in the HSG. For instance: Elliot Philipp, *Childlessness*, Arrow, London, 1975, p. 80:

'it is not painful nor particularly uncomfortable; although nobody claims that it is very pleasant.' John Stangel, *Fertility and Conception*, Paddington, London, 1979, p. 110: '... the uterus becomes slightly stretched and the patient may feel some discomfort. The sensation is usually described as feeling like a moderate menstrual cramp...' Andrew Stanway, *Why Us?*, Granada, St Albans, 1980, p. 130: 'Many women find this test very unpleasant, so doctors give a tranquiliser and painkiller to be taken before the patient attends for the test.' Derek Llewelyn Jones, *Principals of Obstetrics and Gynaecology*, Volume 2, Faber, London, 1978, p. 102: 'Unfortunately it is more inconvenient, costly and painful, as, in general, it should be performed without anaesthesia, although pethidine is given one hour before the investigation.' J.S. Sanfilippo, M.A. Yussman, O. Smith, 'Hysterosalpingogram: A Six Year Review of its Use', *Fertility and Sterility*, 30, 1978, p. 636: 'Pain was reported in 80 per cent of patients undergoing the procedure.' All the women we spoke to found the test either uncomfortable or painful, but only one was offered any painkiller prior to the test.
6. Sanfilippo, Yussman, Smith, *op. cit.*, p. 636.
7. Given how common fibroids are there is little written about them. For a good but brief review see Jill Turner, Wendy Savage, *The Good Health Guide for Women*, British edition, Hamlyn, London, 1981. Veasy C. Buttram, Robert C. Reiter, 'Uterine Leiomyomata, Etiology, Symptomology and Management', *Fertility and Sterility*, 36, 1981, pp. 433–445.
8. For a good review article see Joseph W. Goldzieher, 'Polycystic Ovarian Disease', *Fertility and Sterility*, 35, 1981, pp. 371–390.
9. H.W. Jones Jnr, J.A. Rock, 'Other Factors associated with Infertility: Endometriosis Externa, Fibromyomata Uteri', in R.J. Pepperell, Bryan Hudson, Carl Wood (eds), *The Infertile Couple*, Churchill Livingstone, New York, 1980, pp. 147–158. Leon Speroff, Robert Glass, Nathan Kase, *Clinical Gynaecologic Endocrinology and Infertility*, Williams and Williams, Baltimore, 1978, pp. 355–362. A.D. Noble, A.T. Letchworth, 'Treatment of Endometriosis: A Study of Medical Management', *British Journal of Obstetrics and Gynaecology*, 87, 1980, pp. 726–728.
10. Janet R. Daling, Leon R. Spadoni, Irvin Emanuel, 'Role of Induced Abortion in Secondary Infertility', *Obstetrics and Gynaecology*, 57, 1981 pp. 59–61.
11. For a medical discussion, see A. Lopata, W.I.H. Johnston, J. Leeton, J.C. McBain, 'Use of In Vitro Fertilization in the Infertile Couple', in R.J. Pepperell, Bryan Hudson, Carl Wood (eds), *The Infertile Couple*, Churchill Livingstone, New York, 1980, pp. 209–228.
For a more general discussion, see Peter Williams and Gordon Stevens, 'What Now for Test Tube Babies?', *New Scientist*, 4 February 1982, pp. 312–316. Helen Holmes, Betty Hoskins, Michael Gross (eds), *The Custom Made Child? Women Centred Perspectives*, Humana Press, Clifton, New Jersey, 1980, pp. 259 and 263.

CHAPTER 7: INFERTILITY IN MEN AND WOMEN: COMPATIBILITY

1. See chapter 4, note 16.
2. Jeannine Parvati, *Hygieia: A Woman's Herbal* Wildwood House, London, 1979, chapter 2. Isa Kelso, *Causes and Treatment of Women's Ailments*, Thorsons, third edition, 1973.

CHAPTER 8: MISCARRIAGE AND STILLBIRTH

1. D.J. Begley, J.A. Firth, J.R.S. Hoult, *Human Reproduction and Developmental Biology*, London, Macmillan, 1980, p. 144.

2. Melba Wilson in Stephanie Dowrick and Sibyl Grundberg, *Why Children?*, Women's Press, London, 1980. pp. 113–114.

3. Louise Marsden, 'More than One Womb', *Spare Rib*, 88, November 1979, pp. 24–27. Howard Jones, 'Reproductive Impairment and the Malformed Uterus', *Fertility and Sterility*, 36, 1981, pp. 137–148.

4. Susan Borg, Judith Lasker, *When Pregnancy Fails*, Beacon, Boston, 1981, p. 52.

5. For a discussion of the experience of stillbirth see Liz Standish, 'The Loss of a Baby', *Lancet*, March 13, 1982, pp. 611–612. A. Cartwright, *The Dignity of Labour*, Tavistock, London, 1979, chapter 3.

6. For a clear exposition of the crucial nature of early contact, see M.H. Klaus and J.H. Kennell, *Maternal-Infant Bonding*, Mosby St Louis, 1976. And for a critique of this approach see, for instance, Susan B.G. Campbell and Paul M. Taylor, 'Bonding and Attachment: Theoretical Issues' in Paul M. Taylor (ed), *Parent-Infant Relationships*, New York: Grune and Stratton, 1980. Anne Woollett, David White and Louise Lyon, 'Observations of Fathers at Birth' in Nigel Beail and Jacqueline McGuire (eds), *Fathering: Psychological Perspectives*, London, Junction Books, (1982). Michael Rutter *Maternal Deprivation Reassessed*, Harmondsworth, Penguin, second edition, 1981, pp.201–205.

CHAPTER 9: BECOMING A MOTHER: PREGNANCY, ADOPTION, FOSTERING AND SHARED CHILDCARE

1. For a discussion of having a baby later in life see Janet Price, *You're Not Too Old To Have A Baby*, British edition, Penguin, Harmondsworth, 1979.

2. See Avril Clegg and Anne Woollett, *Twins: From Conception to Five Years*, Century Publishing, 1983.

3. For a discussion of this issue see *Spare Rib* 114, January 1982, p. 26, and *Spare Rib* 115, February 1982, p. 26.

4. For a discussion of these changes in adoption see Barbara Tizard, *Adoption: a Second Chance* Open Books, London, 1977.

5. Sara Maitland, *Daughters of Jerusalem*, Blond and Briggs, London, 1987, p. 74.

6. For discussion of the success of adoption, see p. 160.

7. For a discussion of shared childcare, see a series of articles in *Spare Rib*, 66, January 1978, pp. 14–18; 67, February 1978, pp. 16–18; 68, March 1978, pp. 16–19.

8. Maitland, *op. cit.*, pp. 168.

CHAPTER 10: COPING WITH INFERTILITY

1. For a discussion of grief, see Peter and Diane Houghton, *Unfocussed Grief: Responses to Childlessness* Birmingham Settlement, Birmingham, 1977; Colin Murray-Parkes, *Bereavement: Studies of Grief in Adult Life* Penguin, Harmondsworth, 1975; Barbara E. Menning, *Infertility: A Guide for the Childless Couple* Prentice Hall, New York, 1977.

2. Winifred Holtby, *The Crowded Street*, Virago, London, 1981, p. 269.

3. We found the chapter by Irena Klepfisz in Stephanie Dowrick and Sibyl Grundberg (eds) *Why Children?*, The Women's Press, London, 1980, very stimulating when we were writing this chapter.

4. Anja Meulenbelt, *For Ourselves, Our Bodies and Sexuality – from Women's Point of View*, Sheba, London, 1981, p. 111.

5. The Feminist Insemination Group, *Self Insemination*, London, 1980, p. 33.

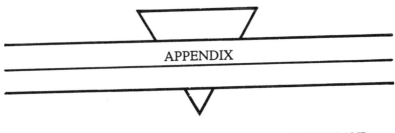

APPENDIX

WHERE TO GO FOR INFORMATION ABOUT INFERTILITY AND INFERTILITY SERVICES

Family Planning Information Service

The Family Planning Association keeps a register of clinics offering infertility services and can tell you which is your nearest clinic. In some cases, they can refer you to clinics. For more information contact your local FPA office whose address and phone number should be in your local telephone directory or contact the national office: 27–35 Mortimer Street, London W1N 7RJ. Tel: 01 636 7866

Community Health Councils

Your local Community Health Council (CHC) may be able to give you information about the infertility services offered by the National Health Service in your area.

If you have any complaints about the service you are getting, then report these to the CHC. Some CHCs have women's groups which you might find are more sympathetic to your complaints about infertility services. For the address and telephone number of your local CHC see your local telephone directory.

Health Education Council

The Health Education Council does not publish any information about infertility or miscarriage. One way, however, to bring these topics to their attention is to contact them and ask them for information. 78 New Oxford Street, London WC1. Tel: 01 637 1881

British Pregnancy Advisory Service (BPAS)

BPAS offers a private service, charging an initial consultation fee and then a fee for treatment. The BPAS is a charity and non-profit making and tries to keep the fees as reasonable as possible. BPAS offers infertility counselling and testing and AID at some of their branches throughout the United Kingdom. For information, contact them at Austy Manor, Wootton Wawen, Solihull, West Midlands B95 6BX. Tel: Henley in Arden 3225

Bourn Hall Clinic

This private clinic was set up by P.C. Steptoe and R.G. Edwards, the pioneers of in-vitro fertilisation. Patients must be referred by their GP or infertility specialist. Bourn Hall, Bourn, Cambridge CB3 7TR. Tel: Cambridge 315955

INFERTILITY SUPPORT GROUPS

National Association for the Childless (NAC)

NAC receives some financial support from the Department of Health and Social Security (DHSS). Its aims are to provide support and information for infertile people. Its members include infertile people and medical professionals who investigate and treat infertility. NAC is organised into regional groups which hold meetings and provide contacts. NAC produces a quarterly newsletter and pamphlets on infertility, including 'Unfocussed Grief' which examines the emotional impact of infertility. Membership costs about £8 a year. 318 Summer Lane, Birmingham B19 3RL. Tel: 021 359 4887

Child

Child is run entirely on a voluntary basis. Its main concern is to collect funds to finance research. The services it provides to members include information sheets on aspects of infertility, a quarterly newsletter and a twenty-four-hour counselling service. Annual membership is about £5. 'Farthings', Gaunts Road, Pawlett, Near Bridgewater, Somerset. Tel: Bridgewater (0278) 683595

Women's Therapy Centre

The Women's Therapy Centre organise short courses on a wide variety of topics around women's emotional health. If sufficient women show interest, they are willing to run one on infertility. They also offer group and individual therapy and can put you in touch with feminist therapists in your area. They charge for all these services, but employ a sliding scale. 6 Manor Gardens, London N7. Tel: 01 263 6200

British Organisation of Non-Parents (BON)

BON represents the views of people who are childless by choice and tries to counter the social pressure to have children by highlighting the positive aspects of a childless existence. BON produces a quarterly newsletter and arranges meetings.
B M Box 5866, London WC1N 3XX

All these organisations are non-profit-making and if you want a reply to your letter, it would help them if you enclosed a stamped addressed envelope.

OTHER USEFUL ADDRESSES

Pill Victims Action Group

This group was set up by women suffering from conditions related to the use of the contraceptive pill, in particular thrombosis. Their aim is to get more information about possible risks of pill use available to women in the UK.
3 Eney Close, Abingdon, Oxfordshire. Tel: 0235 26232

Endometriosis Self-Help Group

This group publishes a newsletter with information about endometriosis and through meetings provides support for women with endometriosis. 65 Holmdene Ave, Herne Hill, London SE24. Tel: 01 737 4764

Stillbirth and Perinatal Death Association

Members of this association include women who have experienced stillbirth or perinatal death and interested medical professionals. The association publishes a newsletter, holds meetings and its members provide emotional support for women throughout the United Kingdom.
37 Christchurch Hill, London NW3 1JY. Tel: 01 794 4601

Women and Work Hazards Group

This group researches and publicises the hazards women are exposed to at their place of work. If you are concerned about the effects of your job on your reproductive health and would like to monitor the effects of certain processes at your place of work on yourself and other women, they can advise you on the best way to do so.
c/o BSSRS, 9 Poland Street, London W1.

Psychosexual Counselling

If you want psychosexual counselling, you can ask your GP to refer you to a clinical psychologist, or you can obtain information about other practitioners from the Marriage Guidance Council, Family Planning Association or the Women's Therapy Centre.

Marriage Guidance Council: 76a New Cavendish Street, London W1. Tel: 01 580 1087

Family Planning Association: 27–35 Mortimer Street, London W1N 7RJ.

Women's Therapy Centre: 6 Manor Gardens, London N7. Tel: 01 263 6200

MEDICAL ALTERNATIVES TO INFERTILITY TREATMENT

Homeopathic: For a list of homeopathic GPs, NHS and private, contact:

The Hahnemann Society: Humane Education Centre, Avenue Lodge, Bounds Green Road, London N22.

For a list of lay practitioners, contact:

The Society of Homeopaths: 101 Sebastian Avenue, Shenfield, Brentwood, Essex.

ADOPTION AND FOSTERING

The British Agencies for Adoption and Fostering (BAAF) produce a number of useful pamphlets about adoption and fostering, including 'Adopting a Child', a guide for adoptive parents which discusses adoption procedures, describes the present adoption situation and gives the names and addresses and the requirements laid down for adoptive parents by adoption agencies and local authorities. This booklet is the obvious place to start if you are considering adoption. Other booklets cover topics such as adopting older children or black children and fostering. 11 Southwark Street, London SE1 1RQ. Tel: 01 407 8800

Agencies actively engaged in finding parents for 'hard to place' children

Parents for Children: 222 Camden High Street, London NW1 8QR.

Adoption Project: Thomas Coram Foundation, 40 Brunswick Square, London WC1 1AZ.

British Agencies for Adoption and Fostering (formerly Adoption Resource Exchange) 11 Southwark Street, London SE1 1RQ. Tel: 01 407 8800.
BAAF produces a booklet 'Be my Parent' which gives information about children who are seeking parents. You can see this book at your local Social Services Department.

Local Authorities
Local authorities are responsible for 'hard to place children' and act as adoption and fostering agencies. Some advertise in newspapers, or you can get their address from your local telephone directory or find it in 'Adopting a Child' from BAAF.

Parent to Parent Information on Adoption Services
This group was formed by parents who had adopted 'hard to place' children. The group offers mutual support and provides information and opportunities for group discussion.
26 Belsize Grove, London NW3.

Overseas Adoption
For information about the legal and practical considerations of adopting children overseas, contact the National Association for the Childless.
318 Summer Lane, Birmingham 19.

Fostering

National Foster Care Association (NFCA)
This is an association of foster parents and others interested in foster care. Francis House, Francis Street, London SW1.

BOOKS TO READ

Books on Infertility
Some of these books are now out of print but you may come across them in your public library. It is important to bear in mind that some of the procedures described in American books differ from the usual British practice. Andrew Stanway, Why Us?, Granada, 1980 A British book written by a medical journalist with the patient in mind. There are some references to how women and men feel about infertility. John Stangel, *Fertility and Conception: an Essential Guide for Childless Couples*, Paddington Press, 1979. An American book written by a doctor specialising in infertility. Tests and treatments are rigorously separated, implying that this is how your investigations will proceed. Each problem is covered in two places, one for tests and another for treatment, which makes for a fair amount of repetition.
Barbara E. Menning, *Infertility: a Guide for the Childless Couple*, Prentice Hall, 1977. An American book written by a woman who has been through infertility investigations herself and therefore recognises the impact of infertility on your life.
Albert Decker and Suzanne Loebl, *We Want to Have a Baby*, Penguin, 1980. An American book written by a doctor and a medical journalist which describes the support groups run at certain American hospitals for infertile people. Otherwise, the medical information is thin.
Elliot Philipp, *Childlessness*, Arrow, 1975. A British book written by a doctor specialising in infertility who emphasises the idea of the patient as part of an

extensive medical team without considering the dynamics of the doctor-patient relationship. Some of the medical information is now out of date but otherwise the description of the tests and treatment is adequate. There is very little consideration of the impact of infertility on the woman.

Robert Newill, *Childless Marriage*, Penguin, 1974 A British book written by a doctor specialising in infertility. Lots of medical information, some of which is now out of date. This doctor blames infertile women for their difficulties which stem either from their excessive desire for a child or because they are 'women's libbers' who are too aggressive. Newill saves his sympathy for the doctors who treat such women.

Hank Pizer and Christine O. Palinski, *Coping with a Miscarriage*, Jill Norman, 1980. An American book written by a doctor and a woman who had several miscarriages. It contains quite a lot of information and discussion of women's feelings.

Ann Oakley, Ann McPherson and Helen Roberts, *Miscarriage*, Fontana, 1983. A British book written by a doctor and two medical sociologists which looks at the causes and treatment of miscarriage and examines women's experiences.

General Books on Women's Health which contain chapters on Infertility

Angela Phillips and Jill Rakusen, *Our Bodies Ourselves*, British edition, Penguin, 1978. Jill Turner and Wendy Savage, *The Good Health Guide for Women*, British edition, Hamlyn 1981. Federation of Feminist Women's Health Centres *How to Stay out of the Gynaecologists Office*, Peace Press Inc, California, 1981.

Other Books of Interest

Adrienne Rich, *Of Woman Born*, Virago, 1977. A moving discussion of the institution and experience of motherhood which acknowledges infertility. Adrienne Rich examines the patriachal control of women's reproductive capacity which manipulates both childbearing and childlessness into negative qualities.

Stephanie Dowrick and Sibyl Grundberg (eds), *Why Children?*, The Women's Press, 1980. Eighteen women describe what lies behind their decision to have or to not have children. There is some fascinating writing about what children mean to different women and about women's experiences of raising their own and other women's children. Anna Wileman writes about her difficulties in conceiving and Melba Wilson describes her experience of miscarriage.

Sara Maitland, *Daughters of Jerusalem*, Blond and Briggs, 1978. An excellent novel about a woman trying to get pregnant which describes her feelings, the reaction of those around her and her experience of infertility investigations.

David Rudkin, *Ashes*, Pluto Plays, 1978. The first part of this play describes graphically the experience of a man and a woman who are trying to have a baby. It contains scenes of having sex to order, of attending the infertility clinic, the disappointment of miscarriage and adoption procedures.

Lesbian Self Insemination Group, 'Self Insemination'. This phamplet describes the experiences and feelings of a group of lesbian women who try to conceive through self-insemination as well providing practical infromation. The section on problems in conceiving is very powerful. This is an optimistic and inspiring pamphlet for all women. It is available from: Box No. 3, 190 Upper Street, London N1.

Books on Sexuality and Psychosexual Problems

Anja Meulenbelt, *For Ourselves: Our Bodies and Sexuality – from Women's Point of View*, Sheba, 1981. A frank and inspiring discussion of women's sexuality which encourages women to reassess their relationship with their body.

Anne Hooper, *The Body Electric*, Virago, 1980. This book charts the progress of six women in a pre-orgasmic group. Fred Belliveau and Lin Richter, *Understanding Human Sexual Inadequacy* Coronet, 1971. J. Heiman, et al, *Becoming Orgasmic: Sexual growth programmes for Women*, Prentice Hall, 1976. A step-by-step programme for inorgasmic heterosexual women written by men!

Books on Adoption

Jane Rowe, *Yours by Choice: A Guide for Adoptive Parents*, RKP, 1969. This book looks at how to set about adoption, questions to ask yourself, how to adjust to your adoptive child (including adolescents) and how to bring up adoptive children.

A number of interesting and accessible books describe studies of adopted children:

Barbara Tizard *Adoption: A Second Chance*, Open Books, 1977. This is a report of a long-term study of children adopted from children's homes after the age of two. The study looked at how the children settled into their new homes, how they fared some time later and the feelings of their adoptive parents. This is an interesting account aimed at both lay people and professionals in adoption, and using quotes from interviews with mothers.

Lois Raynor, *Adoption of Non-White Children*, Allen and Unwin, 1970. In the late 1960s, a project was set up to encourage the adoption of mixed-race children. This book describes that project and reports on its success.

Lois Raynor, *The Adopted Child Comes of Age*, Allen and Unwin, 1980. Over 100 children placed in adoption by the Thomas Coram Institute were contacted when they reached the age of twenty-one. This book describes their experience of adoption and the feelings of their families.

R.J. Simon and M. Altstein, *Transracial Adoption*, Wiley, New York, 1977. This is a report of a study of white American families who had adopted non-white infants, the great majority of whom were happy with the adoption and had experienced few problems because of the child's colour. These findings are discussed in the context of the political implications of white families adopting black children.

J. Seglow, M.L.K. Pringle and P.J. Wedge, *Growing up Adopted*, Macmillan, 1972, and Lydia Lambert and Jane Streather *Children in Changing Families*, Macmillan, 1980. The National Children's Bureau have monitored the lives of a group of children born in a particular week in 1958. The first of their reports examines the children's lives up to the age of seven; the second up to the age of eleven. Both books show that adopted children did as well at school and were as well adjusted as other children of their age, but that they do experience some problems of adjustment as they approach adolescence. Whether these problems are short-lived will be seen when the next report of the children, aged sixteen, is available.

Obtaining these books

Your local library may keep some of these books or may order them for you. A local bookshop may stock some of them or can order them from the publisher. Some of these books can be obtained by post from the following:

Family Planning Association Bookshop: Send for their booklist and a mail order form. 27/35 Mortimer Street, London W1N 7RJ. Tel: 01 636 7866

National Association for the Childless: 318 Summer Lane, Birmingham 19.

Sisterwrite: 190 Upper Street, London N1. Tel: 01 226 9782

INDEX

If you would like to know more about Virago books, write to us
at 41 William IV Street, London WC2N 4DB for a full catalogue.

Please send a stamped addressed envelope

VIRAGO
Advisory Group

Andrea Adam	Zoë Fairbairns
Carol Adams	Carolyn Faulder
Sally Alexander	Germaine Greer
Rosalyn Baxandall (USA)	Jane Gregory
Anita Bennett	Suzanne Lowry
Liz Calder	Jean McCrindle
Beatrix Campbell	Cathy Porter
Angela Carter	Alison Rimmer
Mary Chamberlain	Elaine Showalter (USA)
Anna Coote	Spare Rib Collective
Jane Cousins	Mary Stott
Jill Craigie	Rosalie Swedlin
Anna Davin	Margaret Walters
Rosalind Delmar	Elizabeth Wilson
Christine Downer (Australia)	Barbara Wynn

Give them
the pleasure of choosing
Book Tokens can be bought
and exchanged at most
bookshops

BREAST CANCER

Carolyn Faulder
*A Guide to its Early Detection
and Treatment*

One woman in seventeen develops cancer of the
breast some time in her life. This honest, positive
and reassuring book is Everywoman's guide to
one of the most intimidating health problems she
could ever face. It stresses the importance of
early detection of a cancer, of good
communication between doctor and patient,
explains how early treatment can effect a cure
and reminds women that a lump or cyst is not
necessarily a symptom of malignant cancer. For
those facing or recovering from surgical
treatment, the author offers advice on the
problems of convalescence and readjustment, and
answers the many questions that cause patients
the greatest anxiety.

'Full of helpful good sense . . . Carolyn Faulder
knows her subject well' — *Guardian*

Carolyn Faulder is a journalist and author of
several books, including *Talking to Your Doctor*
and *Treat Yourself to Sex*. She lives in London.